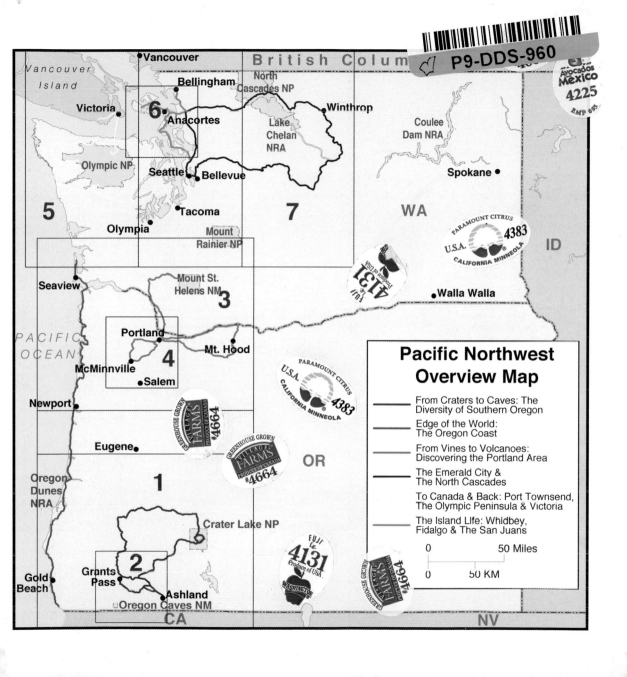

Pacific NW Map 1

- ● Places to Stay
- — From Craters to Caves: The Diversity of Southern Oregon
- — Edge of the World: The Oregon Coast

0 ——————— 20 Miles
0 ——————— 20 KM

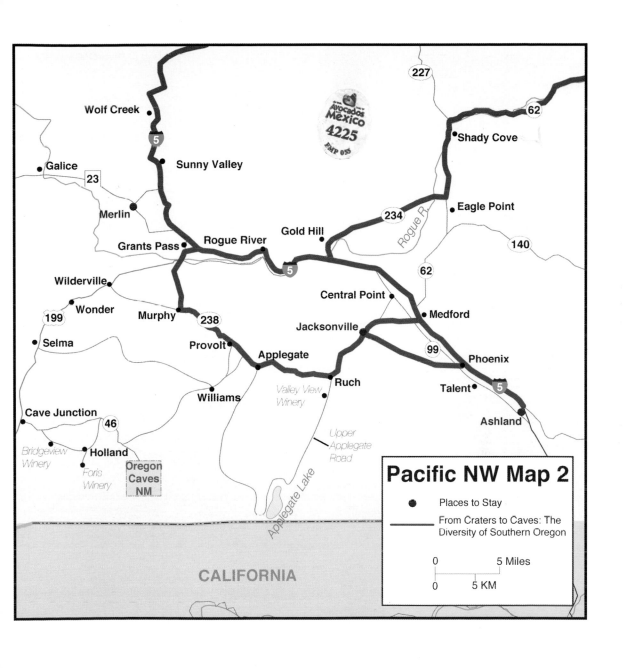

Pacific NW Map 2

● Places to Stay

From Craters to Caves: The Diversity of Southern Oregon

0 — 5 Miles
0 — 5 KM

Leadbetter Point SP
Oysterville
Ocean Park
Long Beach
Seaview
Ilwaco
101
12
706
Mount Rainier NP
508
7
12
5
504
Mount St.
Helens NM
6
4
Castle Rock
Longview
Kelso
Astoria
Fort Clatsop NM
30
Warrenton
Seaside
Cannon Beach
Arch Cape
Manzanita
PACIFIC
101
OCEAN
Oceanside
Tillamook
Sandlake
Pacific City
Neskowin
Lincoln City
Otis
Depoe Bay
Yaquina Head
Newport
101
Waldport
Yachats
Cape Perpetua
22
18
18
22
223
20
34
Corvallis
Albany
228
99
5
Eugene
503
Woodland
St. Helens
Scappoose
26
6
Gaston
47
McMinnville
18
Amity
Tigard
99W
Newberg
Woodburn
Salem
Vancouver
Portland
Troutdale
Corbett
Oregon City
211
22
Lebanon
20
126
141
Hood River
14
84
30
Mosier
Multnomah
Falls
35
26
Mt. Hood
26
Bend

Pacific NW Map 3

● Places to Stay

From Vines to Volcanoes:
Discovering the Portland Area

Edge of the World:
The Oregon Coast

0   20 Miles
0   20 KM

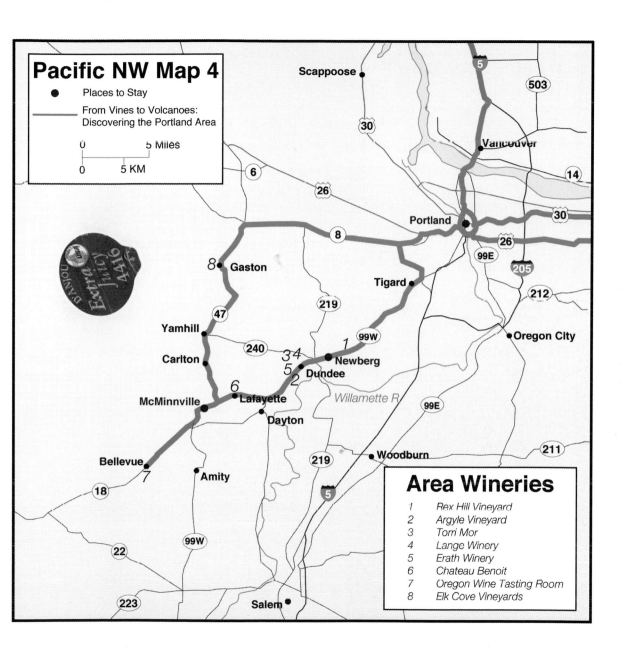

Pacific NW Map 4

- **●** Places to Stay

— From Vines to Volcanoes:
Discovering the Portland Area

0   5 Miles

0   5 KM

Scappoose

503

30

Vancouver

14

Portland

30

26

99E

205

8

212

Gaston 8

Tigard

219

47

99W

Oregon City

Yamhill

240

3 4
Carlton

1

5   Newberg

2 Dundee

6

McMinnville   Lafayette

Willamette R.

99E

Dayton

211

Bellevue

219

Woodburn

7

Amity

5

18

99W

22

223

Salem

Area Wineries

1	Rex Hill Vineyard
2	Argyle Vineyard
3	Torri Mor
4	Lange Winery
5	Erath Winery
6	Chateau Benoit
7	Oregon Wine Tasting Room
8	Elk Cove Vineyards

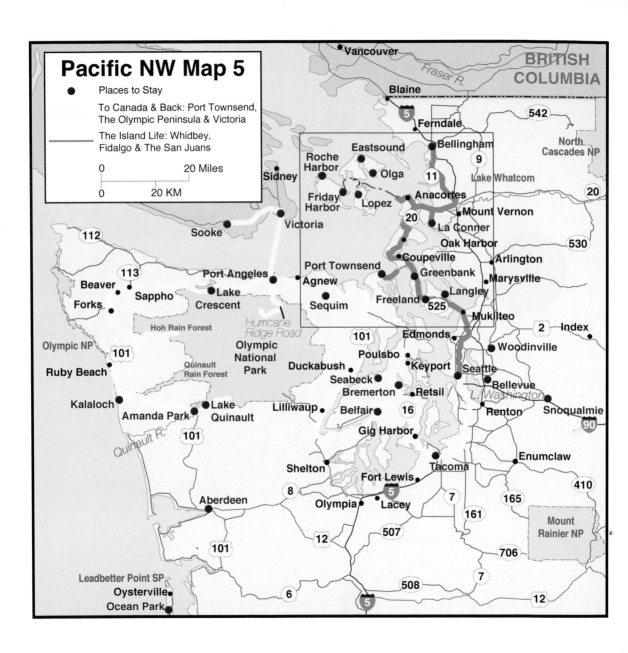

Pacific NW Map 5

- Places to Stay

To Canada & Back: Port Townsend, The Olympic Peninsula & Victoria

The Island Life: Whidbey, Fidalgo & The San Juans

0   20 Miles

0   20 KM

Vancouver

BRITISH COLUMBIA

Fraser R.

Blaine

5

Ferndale

542

North Cascades NP

Eastsound

Bellingham

9

Roche Harbor

Olga

11

Lake Whatcom

Sidney

20

Anacortes

Mount Vernon

530

Friday Harbor

Lopez

20

La Conner

Victoria

Oak Harbor

Arlington

112

Sooke

Port Townsend

Coupeville

Greenbank

Marysville

113

Port Angeles

Agnew

Langley

Beaver

Lake Crescent

Sequim

Freeland

525

Forks

Sappho

Mukilteo

Hoh Rain Forest

Hurricane Ridge Road

101

Edmonds

2

Index

Olympic NP

101

Olympic National Park

Poulsbo

Woodinville

Quinault Rain Forest

Duckabush

Keyport

Seattle

Ruby Beach

Seabeck

Bellevue

Kalaloch

Bremerton

Retsil

L. Washington

Amanda Park

Lake Quinault

Lilliwaup

Belfair

16

Renton

Snoqualmie

101

Quinault R.

Gig Harbor

90

Enumclaw

Shelton

Tacoma

410

Aberdeen

Fort Lewis

8

5

7

165

Olympia

Lacey

161

Mount Rainier NP

12

507

706

7

101

Leadbetter Point SP

Oysterville

6

508

5

12

Ocean Park

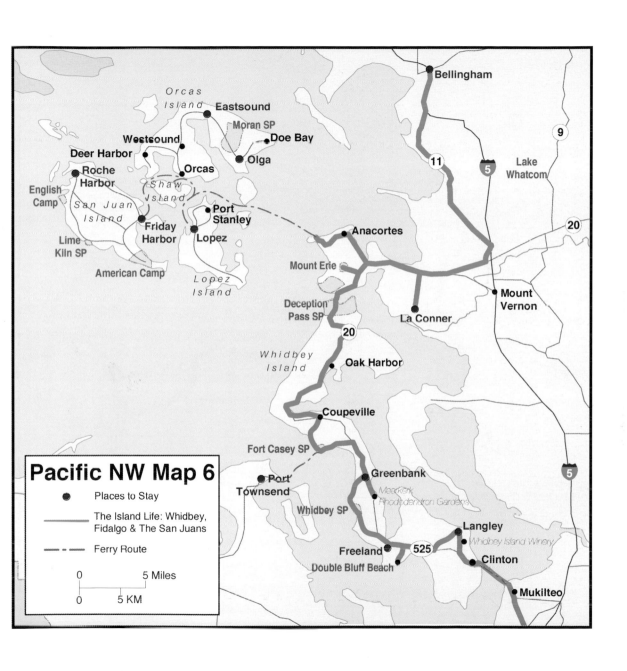

Pacific NW Map 6

- ● Places to Stay
- ─── The Island Life: Whidbey, Fidalgo & The San Juans
- ─·─ Ferry Route

| 0 | | 5 Miles |
| 0 | | 5 KM |

Bellingham

9

11

5

Lake Whatcom

20

Orcas Island

Eastsound

Moran SP

Doe Bay

Westsound

Deer Harbor

Orcas

Olga

Roche Harbor

Shaw Island

English Camp

San Juan Island

Port Stanley

Friday Harbor

Lopez

Lime Kiln SP

American Camp

Lopez Island

Anacortes

Mount Erie

Mount Vernon

Deception Pass SP

La Conner

20

Whidbey Island

Oak Harbor

20

5

Coupeville

Fort Casey SP

Port Townsend

Greenbank

Meerkerk Rhododendron Gardens

Whidbey SP

Langley

Whidbey Island Winery

Freeland

525

Clinton

Double Bluff Beach

Mukilteo

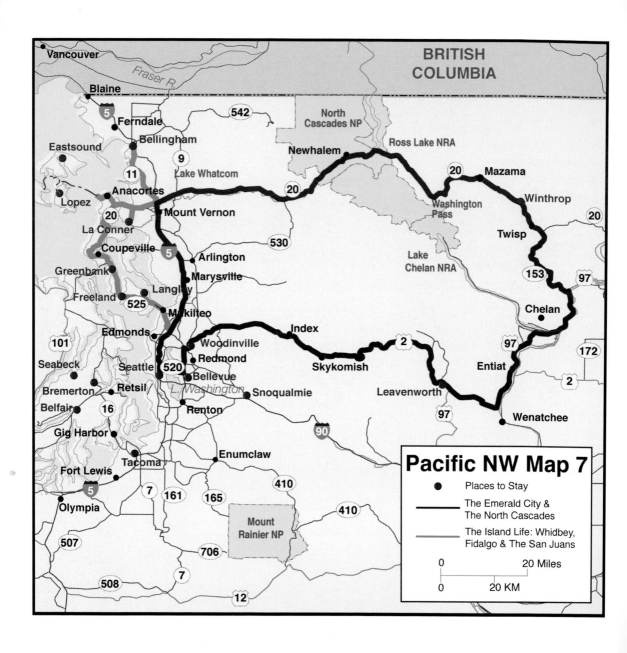

Karen Brown's
PACIFIC NORTHWEST
2007

Colette's Bed & Breakfast, Port Angeles

Contents

Dedicated to my faithful brother
John Francis
My Sherpa, my stalwart, my "steady on"

Beth Knutsen

Cover Painting: Colette's Bed & Breakfast, Port Angeles, Washington.

Authors: Karen Brown, June Eveleigh Brown, Beth Knutsen.
Editors: Clare Brown, Karen Brown, June Eveleigh Brown, Debbie Tokumoto.
Illustrations: Vanessa Kale Brown.
Cover painting: Jann Pollard.
Maps: Michael Fiegel and Rachael Kircher-Randolph.
Technical support: Gary Meisner.
Copyright © 2007 by Karen Brown's Guides.

Distributed by National Book Network, 15200 NBN Way, Blue Ridge Summit, PA 17214, USA. Tel: 717-794-3800 or 1-800-462-6420, Fax: 1-800-338-4500, Email: custserv@nbnbooks.com

A catalog record for this book is available from the British Library.

ISSN 1539-9915

Introduction

Mount Rainier

Welcome to the Pacific Northwest, a fresh and captivating corner of North America, where Nature gives us a glimpse at her incomprehensible range. Here, a fusion of vastly different topographies comes together in one unlikely painting: endless stretches of windswept, sandy beaches; dense expanses of sylvan forest; great crashing rivers; dramatic river valleys; gently rolling hills covered in neat rows of vines; the portentous presence of towering, snow-capped volcanoes; and vast high deserts of sagebrush and juniper, still bearing witness to the largest voluntary land migration in recorded history. This is a place where Nature reigns, a place where man still treads with a reverent step. It's a casual, no-nonsense, friendly place—even in the cities of Portland, Seattle, and Victoria.

In our guide covering this magnificent corner of the world, we'll visit some of the most inviting places in Oregon and Washington States and to the very southern tip of Vancouver Island in British Columbia. (By the way, say OR-ih-gun, not OR-ih-gone. No one seems certain where the state name came from, but it's many an historian's guess that it comes from the French *ouragan*, meaning storm.) The great Northwest includes many amazing regions that we don't cover yet, but we'll make up for that in future editions. For our most up-to-date research, it's always best to check in regularly at our website: *www.karenbrown.com*. In addition to six unique driving itineraries designed to make the most of your travel time, we offer you our personal recommendations for great places to stay. After all, we know that where you lay your head each night makes the difference between a good or a *great* vacation.

About Itineraries

The itineraries are outlined on the maps highlighting hotel locations found at the front of the book in the Color Map Section and additionally on the more detailed, black and white map preceding each itinerary. The Color Overview Map will help you visualize the routings of the various itineraries as they navigate a course through the Pacific Northwest States. Tailor these itineraries to meet your own specific needs by leaving out some sightseeing if time is limited, or linking several itineraries together if you wish to enjoy a longer vacation.

For detailed trip planning, it is essential to supplement these with comprehensive commercial maps. Rand McNally maps are available for purchase on our website, *www.karenbrown.com*. Each route can be tailored to meet your own individual vision.

CANADIAN TRAVEL

The exchange rate in Canada favors the traveler from the United States particularly. This is a great opportunity to splurge! Citizens of the U.S. need proof of citizenship, so carry a valid passport *or* be prepared to present a driver's license with *either* a copy of your birth certificate *or* a voter's registration card. Visitors from all other countries must have a valid passport and, in some cases, a visa. If you are in doubt about the appropriate travel documents, contact the Canadian embassy or consulate office nearest you. There's no need to worry about vaccinations.

CAR RENTAL

Our itineraries are designed for travel by car. Three itineraries for Washington State (including one that incorporates a trip to Victoria, British Columbia) begin and end in Seattle, where rentals are easy to arrange. Similarly for our Oregon itineraries you will have no trouble picking up a car in Ashland or Portland. Since all three towns are easy to get around in on foot or by public transportation, it might be practical to wait until you have done all your city sightseeing before renting a car. When making arrangements to rent, be sure to let the car rental company know where you plan to travel—sometimes there are restrictions on traveling to Canada.

GASOLINE

Please make note: In the state of Oregon, there is no self-serve option at gasoline stations. So sit back, relax, and let the attendants do all the work for you. It's the *law!*

MAPS

A total of eight colored maps are to be found at the front of the book. The Overview Map outlines our recommended driving itineraries as they cross through the Pacific Northwest States. The Overview Map is followed by a series of more detailed maps that show the itinerary routings and all the towns in which we have recommended a place to stay by geographic state groupings. Preceding each itinerary is a black-and-white map that outlines the suggested route, detailing the sightseeing suggestions and roads. These maps are simple renderings and not always to scale. Again, for detailed trip planning, it is essential to supplement these with comprehensive commercial maps. Rand McNally maps are available on our website, *www.karenbrown.com.*

PACING

At the beginning of each itinerary we suggest pacing. The time frames we suggest reflect how much there is to see and do. Use these recommendations as guidelines only. Craft your own itinerary based on how much leisure time you have and whether your preference is to move on to a new destination each day or settle in and use a particular inn as base.

WEATHER

Temperatures in this part of the country are mild compared to most other regions in the U.S., but some areas are more prone to rain or drizzle than others. In general, you can count on it growing cooler and wetter the farther north you travel; and drier and warmer the farther inland. Southwestern Oregon, for example, gets about 70 inches of rain each year, mostly between October and May. Its summers are quite hot. Compare that to the Olympic Peninsula in western Washington, which gets between 130 and 200 inches of rain annually! Mountain ranges—the Coast Range and the Cascades—run in a north/south pattern through the Northwest and have a profound effect on the weather. Areas west of these ranges are wetter and cooler; while areas east of the mountains tend to be hot and dry, since moisture-heavy clouds are depleted of their loads by the time they cross the mountains as they head east to the ocean. Freezing temperatures are rare, except in the mountains. Overall, it doesn't rain as much as you hear. Seattle, for example, has a reputation for frequent gray skies; while, in fact, it records only about 38 inches of rain each year. In dressing for the weather here, the layering approach is best—and pack a windbreaker for the islands and the coast.

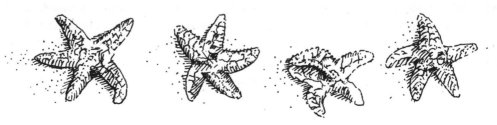

About Inn Travel

We use the term "inn" to cover everything from a simple bed and breakfast to a sophisticated resort. A wide range of inns is included in this guide: some are great bargains, others very costly; some are in cities or well-trafficked areas, others in remote locations; some are quite sophisticated, others extremely simple. The common denominator is that each place has some special quality that makes it appealing. Our descriptions are intended to give you an honest appraisal of each property, so that you can select an accommodation based on your personal preferences. The following pointers will help you appreciate and understand what to expect when traveling the "inn" way.

AFFILIATIONS:

If a property is a member of either Select Registry or Relais & Châteaux we reference this on the hotel description page.

BATHROOMS

We do not specify whether the bath is equipped with stall-shower, tub-shower, tub only, or Jacuzzi, so you'll need to ask when you make your reservation. Some inns offer guestrooms that share a bath with other rooms, or rooms that have a private bath but locate it down the hall so you'll need to ask about that, too.

BREAKFAST

Breakfast is usually included in the room rate, and we make note if it is not. Although innkeepers take great pride in their morning offerings, know that breakfast can range from a gourmet "waddle-away" feast (as proudly described by one innkeeper-chef) to muffins and coffee. Sometimes breakfast is limited to a Continental in your room or is a hot breakfast with others in the dining room, and sometimes both. Breakfast times vary as well—some innkeepers serve a hot breakfast at a specified time, while others replenish a buffet on a more leisurely schedule. Breakfasts are as unique as the inns themselves.

CANCELLATION POLICIES

Although policies vary, inns are usually more rigorous than large chain hotels about their cancellation policies. Understand their terms when securing a reservation.

CHARM

It is very important to us that an inn has charm. Ideally, an inn should be appealing in several ways: perhaps in an historic building, tastefully decorated, lovingly managed, and in a wonderful location. Few inns meet every criterion, but all our selections have something that makes them special and are situated in memorable surroundings. (We have had to reject several lovely inns because of a poor location.) Small inns are usually our favorites, but size alone does not dictate whether or not a hostelry is chosen.

CHECK-IN

Inns are usually very specific about check-in time—generally between 3 and 6 pm. Let your innkeeper know if you are going to arrive late so that (s)he can make special arrangements, such as leaving a door key and a note with directions to your room under a potted plant. Also, for those who might wish to arrive early, note that some inns close their doors between check-out and check-in times. Inns are frequently staffed only by the owners themselves, and that window of time between check-out and check-in is often the only opportunity to shop for those wonderful breakfasts they prepare in addition to running their own personal errands.

CHILDREN

Many places in this guide do not welcome children. Inns cannot legally refuse accommodation to children but, as parents, we really want to stay where our children are genuinely welcome, so ask when making reservations. In the inn descriptions on our website (*www.karenbrown.com*) we have an icon that indicates at what age children are welcome.

COMFORT

As important as charm is, comfort plays a deciding role in the selection of inns we recommend. Firm mattresses, a quiet setting, good lighting, fresh towels, scrubbed bathrooms—we do our best to remember the basics when considering inns. The charming decor and innkeeper will soon be forgotten, if you do not enjoy a good night's sleep and comfortable stay.

CREDIT CARDS

Whether or not an establishment accepts credit cards is indicated in the list of icons at the bottom of each description by the symbol ▆. We have also specified which cards are accepted as follows: None, AX–American Express, MC–MasterCard, VS–Visa, or simply, all major.

FOOD

The majority of places featured in this guide do not have restaurants, but innkeepers are always very knowledgeable about and happy to recommend local favorites. Most inns do serve breakfast and, quite often, a sumptuous one. Frequently in addition to breakfast, tea or wine and hors d'oeuvres are served in the afternoon or evening, either at a specific time or on a self-serve basis at your leisure. Sometimes, if you request it in advance, a picnic lunch can also be prepared.

If you have any special dietary requirements, most innkeepers will gladly try to accommodate you. Not having the resources a restaurant would have, they usually plan a breakfast menu that features one entrée, making sure to have the necessary ingredients on hand. It is best to mention any special requirements at the time you make your reservation, both as a courtesy and from a practical point of view. The innkeeper will want the chance to stock items, such as low-fat dairy products, egg substitutes, sugar-free syrups, etc.

ICONS

We have introduced these icons in the guidebooks and there are more on our website, *www.karenbrown.com.* ❄ Air conditioning in rooms, ⊤ Beach nearby, ☕ Breakfast included in room rate, ⚘ Children welcome, ♨ Cooking classes offered, ▭ Credit cards accepted, ☎ Direct-dial telephone in room, 🐕 Dogs by special request, ⛪ Elevator, 🏋 Exercise room, ♨ Fireplaces in some bedrooms, Ⴘ Mini-refrigerator in rooms, **P** Parking available, ¶¶ Restaurant, ⊘ Some non-smoking rooms, ⚘ Spa, ≈ Swimming pool, ⚡ Tennis, 🖵 Television with English channels, ⚘ Wedding facilities, ♿ Wheelchair friendly, ⚑ Golf course nearby, 🏃 Hiking trails nearby, 🐎 Horseback riding nearby, ⚡ Skiing nearby, ⚓ Water sports nearby, ⚑ Wineries nearby.

Icons allow us to provide additional information about our recommended properties. When using our website to supplement the guides, positioning the cursor over an icon will, in many cases, give you further details.

RESERVATIONS

The two best ways to make a reservation are to: telephone or (if an inn participates in our website) to contact them via their email hyperlink. If you phone, try not to call during breakfast hours. Also, inns are often homes, so late-night calls are not appreciated. Another convenient and efficient way to request a reservation is by fax. When planning your trip, be aware that many inns require a two-night stay on weekends and over holidays. Note: Discounted midweek and off-season rates are often available, so do ask about them.

ROOM RATES

Rates can vary often between high-season, low-season, midweek, weekend, and holiday pricing. We have quoted only high-season rates for 2007 generally a range from the lowest-priced bedroom for two people (singles usually receive a very small discount) to the most expensive suite, including breakfast. The rates given are those quoted to us by the inn. In Canada (Sooke and Victoria) we quote Canadian dollars. Please use these figures as a guideline, and be certain to ask what the rates are and what they include.

We have not given prices for "special" rooms, such as those that can accommodate three people traveling together. Discuss options with the innkeeper. We make a note of all exceptions, e.g., when an inn does not include breakfast with the price of your room. The rates we quote do not include tax.

SMOKING

Most inns have an extremely strict non-smoking policy. A few inns permit smoking in restricted public areas or outside, but in general, it is best to assume that smoking is not appropriate. If you need a place where smoking is allowed, be sure to ask the hotel about the specifics of their policy.

SOCIALIZING

Inns usually offer a conviviality rarely found in a "standard" hotel. The gamut runs from intimate gatherings around the kitchen table to sharing a sophisticated, elegant cocktail hour in the parlor. Breakfast may be a formal meal served at a set hour when the guests gather around the dining-room table, or it may be served buffet-style over several hours where guests have the option to sit down and eat alone or join other guests at a larger table. Some inns will bring a breakfast tray to your room.

After check-in, many inns offer afternoon refreshment, such as tea and cakes or wine and hors d'oeuvres, which may be seen as another social opportunity. Some inns set out the refreshments buffet-style, where guests are invited to meander in and out, mixing or not mixing with other guests as they choose; while others orchestrate a more structured gathering, often a social hour, with the innkeeper presiding. Choose the inn that seems to offer the degree of privacy that you desire. It's entirely possible to find inns that downplay the social aspect of your visit, if privacy is what you're after.

WEBSITE

Please supplement this book by looking at the information provided on our Karen Brown Website (*www.karenbrown.com*), which serves as an added dimension to our guides. Most of our favorite inns are featured on the site (web participation is an inn's choice) and on their web page you can usually link to their email so that making reservations is a breeze. Also featured on our site are comments, feedback, and discoveries from you, our readers; information on our latest finds; post-press updates; contest drawings for free books; special offers; unique features, such as recipes and favorite destinations; and special savings offered by certain inns.

WHEELCHAIR ACCESSIBILITY

If an inn has *at least* one guestroom that is accessible by wheelchair, it is noted with the symbol ♿. This is not the same as saying it meets full ADA standards.

ZONING LAWS

All major cities impose specific zoning standards on private homes that double as bed and breakfast establishments. The cities of Seattle, Washington and Victoria, British Columbia are particularly exacting about these standards. Please keep in mind that Karen Brown's Guides is not responsible for checking the certification status of recommended properties.

A Final Tip...

CELLPHONE COVERAGE

More and more travelers rely on cellphones to keep in touch with home and office, or to communicate with inns along the way. Keep in mind that cellphone coverage is spotty, at best, along all mountain passes, as well as on the islands in Washington State. Don't rely on uninterrupted coverage at all times in all places.

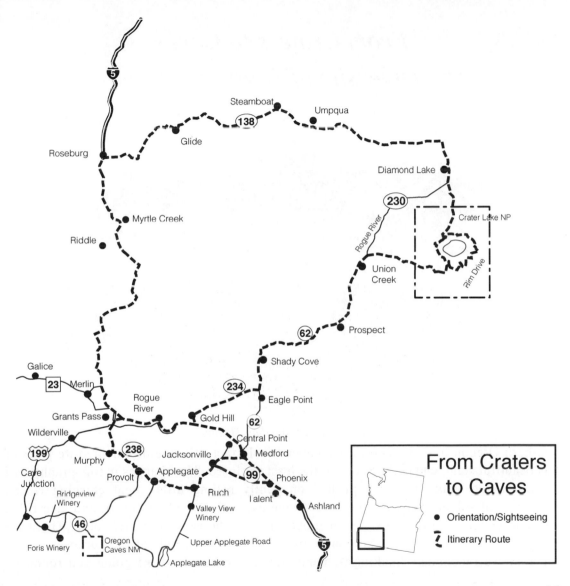

From Craters to Caves

- Orientation/Sightseeing
- Itinerary Route

11

From Craters to Caves
The Diversity of Southern Oregon

Ashland's Elizabethan Theatre

Southern Oregon has so much to recommend it. In fact, it's one of our favorite parts of this beautiful state, and perhaps one of the least explored. The changes in topography will alone astound you: vineyards planted on gently rolling hills, great crashing rivers, labyrinths of subterranean marble caves, huge expanses of sylvan forest, and lake-filled volcanic craters 6 miles wide, to name but a few of the natural marvels here. There are many ways to approach the exploration of this diverse area but for the purposes of this itinerary we recommend making Ashland your home base and we guide you round its many delights. From there we visit a few local wineries, take you on a scenic drive through the Applegate Valley, and on to the Oregon Caves National Monument. We'll also explore the beautiful Rogue River Valley, Crater Lake, and the Umpqua National Forest.

Recommended Pacing: If you try all or even most of the recommendations in this section, you will very easily fill an entire week (seven days); especially if you devote at least two nights for theatergoing at the Oregon Shakespeare Festival and spend three days exploring Ashland. The Applegate Valley tour, with a visit to historic Jacksonville and a local winery, is an easy half-day or day-long loop, but it would better to take two days if you decide to continue on to the Oregon Caves and the Holland Loop wineries. The Rogue/Crater Lake/Umpqua trip is spectacular, so you won't want to rush it: we recommend at least two full days to cover the entire loop. For example, one day to get from Ashland to Steamboat—assuming that you bypass Crater Lake or take only our abbreviated visit to it—and a second day to get from Steamboat back to Ashland. However, if you are pressed for time, Crater Lake is an easy day trip—up and back the same way from Ashland.

ASHLAND

Perhaps best known for its award-winning Oregon Shakespeare Festival, **Ashland** is a thoroughly charming place: a small town and culturally sophisticated destination spot. Occupying a corner in the gentle Rogue River Valley, it is protected between the magnificent Siskiyou and Cascade mountain ranges. It's conveniently located only 15 miles south of the **Medford/Rogue Valley International Airport**, served by both United Airlines and Horizon Air, and is an easy 5½- to 6-hour drive north from San Francisco, or 4 to 5 hours south from Portland via I-5. You'll have no trouble finding stellar accommodations in this town—it's where some of Oregon's finest inns are located. We were hard pressed to end our listings where we did! This is a walking town, to be sure. Take all the time you want to discover parks, bookstores, cafés, boutique shops, and galleries.

The gem that is the **Oregon Shakespeare Festival (OSF)**, located at 15 S. Pioneer Street, is not to be missed. Operating nine months of the year (from February through October, with the outdoor theater open from June), OSF presents both classic *and* contemporary plays in repertory, using Shakespeare as its standard. Plays are performed most days of the week in three theaters simultaneously: the contemporary **Angus Bowmer** (named after the drama professor who started the festival in 1935), the intimate **Black Swan**, and the open-air **Elizabethan Theatre**, designed to look like England's fine old Globe Theater. Since the festival is enormously popular, performances sell out months in advance. Don't let that discourage you from showing up even at the last minute, however. Some of our best success stories occurred when we arrived at the box office on the morning or the evening of a performance, taking advantage of the inevitable cancellations and no-shows. The **Festival Box Office** is very professionally run—let the folks who work there give you tips on how to increase your chances of getting in at the last minute. (Open Monday from 9:30 am to 5 pm, and Tuesday to Sunday from 9:30 am to 8:30 pm; 541-482-4331, *www.osfashland.org*.) Many inns are within easy walking distance of the festival grounds and the downtown area, so park your car once, pick up an OSF schedule, and revel in all you can accomplish on foot!

A wonderful variety of extra activities are scheduled at OSF every week: backstage tours (this is especially fun at the Elizabethan Theatre), informal chats with the actors, lectures by the directors or "dramaturgs," and in summer, an always-enchanting pre-performance show in the main courtyard. At the corner of Pioneer and East Main you'll find the **Festival Exhibit Center**, showcasing costumes, props, audio and video footage from the earliest performances, and over 60 years of photographs. (Open Tuesday to Sunday from 10:30 am to 1:30 pm, mid-February to October.)

Directions to the OSF grounds: Coming from the north on Main Street, turn right on Pioneer. From the south, take Siskiyou Blvd, which veers right to become Lithia Way as it nears the festival grounds. Turn left on Pioneer.

Lithia Park occupies about 100 acres adjacent to the Shakespeare Festival grounds. It's a lovely place to stroll between shows. Notice the drinking fountains in **Lithia Plaza**, which is surrounded by restaurants and shops, but be careful which fountain you choose for a drink! Some produce a sulfurous, lithium-laden mineral water that bubbles up just east of the city, and it's definitely an acquired taste. Early Ashlanders had hoped to build a world-class spa around the local lithium springs, but the idea never quite took off.

There are many excellent delis and bakeries in town, perfect for stocking up on picnic fare. Ask your innkeeper for recommendations. **Chateaulin Fine Wines & Gourmet Foods**, for example, presents a marvelous high-end assortment of pâtés, cheeses, and wines. It's located at 50 E. Main Street next to Chateaulin Restaurant Français. (Open daily from 11 am to 6 pm.)

Now ranking number ten of the "Best Small Art Towns in America" according to the Ashland Gallery Association (AGA), Ashland boasts an intriguing assortment of art galleries. **First Friday Gallery Walking Tours** (from 5 to 8 pm on the first Friday of every month) are becoming more and more popular, as is the annual **Taste of Ashland Walking Tour** in spring. You can meet artists in a casual atmosphere while sampling a local red from the Rogue Valley's best wineries as you amble through galleries downtown and in the Historic Railroad District. Phone the AGA at 877-752-6278 for details. The city is also very proud of its **Schneider Museum of Art** on the University of Southern Oregon campus. Facilities include four small galleries where a broad range of exhibitions is presented. (1250 Siskiyou Blvd; open from 10 am to 4 pm Tuesday to Saturday; and till 7 pm on the first Friday of each month; 541-552-6245, *www.sou.edu/schneider.html.*)

The Ashland area is one of the oldest wine-producing regions in the western U.S., a history that began as far back as the 1840s when immigrant Italians and Swiss, fresh off the Oregon Trail, decided to grow grapes and bottle wine here. Today, the Rogue Valley, where hot days and cool nights create the perfect climate for Bordeaux varietals, produces some excellent red wines. Let's visit a couple of these wineries.

From downtown, head south on Siskiyou Blvd About 4 miles from the Shakespeare Festival Center, turn right at **Weisinger's Vineyard & Winery**. Stroll up to the tasting room and prepare for the friendliest of welcomes. Family-owned and -operated, the Weisinger Vineyard produces all its wines from grapes grown in southern Oregon. Bordeaux varietals are available here, as well as Gewürztraminer, Chardonnay, Pinot, an exotic Italian blend called Mescolare, and many other fine wines. Step out onto the deck and enjoy the mountain views. Browse through the gift shop-deli and consider assembling a picnic lunch to take with you. (3150 Siskiyou Blvd; open from 10 am to 6 pm, May to October; and from 11 am to 5 pm, November to April; 541-488-5989, *www.weisingers.com*.)

Leaving Weisinger's, head north on Siskiyou Blvd, back in the direction of the town center. Turn right on Crowson Road, then left at the dead end onto 66, again in the direction of downtown. Turn right on East Main. Drive ¾ mile and turn right at the **Ashland Vineyards** sign, onto 120 acres of private land—60 of them planted with some ten different types of grapes. Ashland Vineyards has been in business since 1987. The tasting room here is very simple, but Phil and Kathy Kodak will take great pleasure in introducing you to their award winners, and you'll also have a chance to taste their second label, Griffin Creek. (2775 E. Main Street; open April 1 to October 31, Tuesday to Sunday, from 11 am to 5 pm; 541-488-0088; *www.winenet.com*.)

To return to Ashland, turn right on East Main as you leave Ashland Vineyards, and head back to town through residential areas, ending up on Lithia Way.

APPLEGATE VALLEY SCENIC DRIVE

This loop takes you through some lovely countryside to historic Jacksonville, then on to a local winery to sample some of Southern Oregon's finest wines; with the option of then either heading back to Ashland via Grants Pass, or continuing on to the Oregon Caves and another two wineries.

From Ashland, head north on E. Main, which becomes N. Main, then Hwy 99. Just past the town of Phoenix, turn left on South Stage Road and follow the well-placed signage for 6½ miles to historic **Jacksonville**, population barely over 2,000. The short stretch of rural road leading you to town is absolutely lovely: rolling hills, pear and apple orchards, ranches, and well-manicured vineyards. In 1851, two prospectors en route to California discovered gold unexpectedly along a creek in this area, and by 1853, little Jacksonville had become the county seat. Farmers, merchants, bankers, and saloon innkeepers prospered. The Oregon-California Stagecoach Line ensured lots of traffic to keep the budding economy strong, but in 1884 the railroad replaced the stage and bypassed Jacksonville altogether. Adding insult to injury, the county seat moved to Medford in 1927 and Jacksonville was doomed to obscurity. In 1978, however, the town was recognized as a National Historic Landmark District on the National Historic Register and today is Oregon's most extensive and complete example of a late 19th-century mining community. Only eight towns in the whole U.S. carry this distinction. Walking tours past historic sites are detailed in brochures that you can collect at the **Information Center** at the Rogue River Valley Railway Depot, corner of Oregon and

Jacksonville

"C" Streets. (May to September hours: Monday to Friday from 10 am to 5 pm, weekends from noon to 4 pm; all other times of year: Monday to Friday from 10 am to 4 pm, Saturdays from noon to 4 pm; 541-899-8118, *www.jacksonvilleoregon.org*.) Park your car and stroll up and down the streets. The town is very small, so it's easy to get around on foot. Be sure to visit the unusual **Jacksonville Cemetery**, where plots are clustered by religious denomination, including Jewish, Masonic, and Catholic sections. The first burial took place here in 1859.

Each year from mid-June to September, Jacksonville hosts **The Britt Festivals** (*www.brittfest.org*), long considered the Pacific Northwest's premiere outdoor summer performing arts festival. Britt presents dozens of summer concerts, featuring world-class artists in jazz, folk, country, pop, dance, and classical music. Its performance venue is a naturally formed amphitheater set among majestic ponderosa pines on the beautiful hillside estate of 19th-century photographer Peter Britt. Tens of thousands of music lovers travel from all over the West to enjoy Britt's high-energy performances and casual, relaxing atmosphere. The grounds are located downtown at Fir and 1st Streets. Box office numbers are 541-773-6077 and 800-882-7488.

About 9 miles southwest of Jacksonville on Hwy 238, turn left in the town of **Ruch** onto Upper Applegate Road, drive 1 mile, and turn right onto the **Valley View Winery** property. Enjoy a glass of wine among rose bushes in the garden area overlooking the vineyard. Originally established in the mid-1850s by Peter Britt of Britt Festivals fame (see above), Valley View Winery is owned and operated by the delightful Wisnovksy family, who has cleverly transformed a pole barn into a winery and tasting room. Because the Applegate Valley is considerably sunnier, warmer, and drier than elsewhere in western Oregon, Valley View can specialize in grapes that grow best under these conditions: Cabernet Sauvignon, Merlot, Chardonnay, Syrah, and Cabernet Franc. The Anna Maria label, which represents the finest wines they make, is also available for tasting. (1000 Upper Applegate Road; open daily from 11 am to 5 pm; 541-899-8468; *www.valleyviewwinery.com*.)

Leaving the winery, return to 238 west and continue down a narrow two-lane road through more of the lush and gentle Rogue River Valley surrounded by national forests. As you enter Murphy, watch for signs leading you to Grants Pass as Hwy 238 turns and begins to head north. (Skip to the next paragraph now if you will not be extending your tour of the area. Otherwise, continue on to Grants Pass.) **Grants Pass** was once a stopping point on the Oregon-California Stagecoach Line. It got its name in 1863 when settlers building the main road through town got news that Ulysses S. Grant had captured Vicksburg. The town is now a central point for many downriver (the Rogue) rafting trips and a good place to inquire about them. Some 40 miles of the **Rogue River** from Grants Pass to Gold Beach at the Pacific Ocean are protected within the Siskiyou National Forest, where the only access is by foot or raft. For more information about supervised and unsupervised opportunities to explore this gorgeous stretch of river, call the **Siskiyou National Forest Service** at 541-471-6500. River rafting trips generally run from May through October.

Take 238 through Grants Pass and pick up I-5 South (a particularly beautiful stretch of freeway) to return to Ashland.

Option: Oregon Caves and Holland Loop Wineries

Note: If you choose this extended version of the trip, you might consider spending the night at an inn in Jacksonville or Merlin (see listings).

In Murphy, cross a small green bridge over the Applegate River to continue on to the Oregon Caves and Holland Loop. Turn left on New Hope Road in the direction of Wilderville, then in about 3½ miles turn left on Fish Hatchery Road, following signs to Wilderville/Hwy 199. *Look sharp and carry a good area map: these signs are very subtle*. Wend your way through tiny towns, green pasturelands, llama farms, and horse ranches. Beautiful! When Fish Hatchery dead ends after 6½ miles, turn left, then left again onto Hwy 199 South in the direction of Cave Junction. Turn left off Hwy 199 going south onto 46/Oregon Caves National Monument.

You have a couple of choices at this point. A visit to the **Oregon Caves National Monument** will be an unusual treat for anyone who has never experienced a limestone/marble cave before. Keep in mind that cave tours are not for the claustrophobic! The monument's elevation of 4,000 feet plus the necessity to maneuver many hundreds of steps inside the cave (there's a vertical rise of about 218 feet), make the tour strenuous for some. The complete tour lasts about 75 minutes and covers half a mile. It is narrow, low, and damp with temperatures running in the 40s. Wear good shoes and warm clothes and enjoy the adventure! Hours vary—call 541-592-2100, *www.nps.gov/orca*. The **Visitor Center** is located on Hwy 46 as you head east to the caves themselves so stop there first to orient yourself and ask questions.

Now that you're here in the Illinois River Valley, consider a jaunt along the 7-mile **Holland Loop** to visit two of the area's wineries. Keep in mind that these tasting rooms are still fairly simple compared with others but don't let that stop you from experiencing the delights of this out-of-the-way countryside winery. To take the winery tour, you'll turn right on Holland Loop Road off of Hwy 46, not far from where it joins 199 and *before* the Oregon Caves Visitor Center. On the Loop Road, drive 2 miles to **Bridgeview Vineyards and Winery**. Follow the gravel road to the tasting room which is set on a deck overlooking a well-manicured vineyard and a lake stocked with trout, where many a Canadian goose or swan takes up residence, too. Bridgeview is a family-run business, like most of the wineries in the area, and the staff will greet you warmly. Robert and Lelo Kerivan first arrived here in 1979, closely followed by their son, winemaker, René Eichmann, in 1980. The winery you see today was completed in 1986. Reflective of the family's German heritage, its 75 acres are densely planted in the European style of vine spacing to grow Pinot Noir, Chardonnay, Pinot Gris, Riesling, Gewürztraminer, Müller Thurgau, and Early Muscat. In 1998, Bridgeview added a 100-acre vineyard in the Applegate Valley to plant Merlot and other Bordeaux varietals. Meticulous attention to pruning ensures that each vine produces fewer grapes with correspondingly greater varietal character. (4210 Holland Loop Road; call for tasting hours: 541-592-4688 or 877-273-4843; *www.bridgeviewwine.com.*)

Leaving Bridgeview, get back on the Loop Road, then turn right on Kendall. Follow signs to the remote **Foris Vineyards Winery**. With the distinctive honor of being the Pacific Northwest's most southern winery, Foris is situated on the back terrace of the Illinois River Valley. It's almost hidden in the Siskiyou Mountains, so the road to it is half the fun. Varieties produced include Pinot Noir, Chardonnay, Gewürztraminer, and Early Muscat, alongside some wonderful Cabernet and Merlot that come from vineyards located elsewhere within the Rogue Valley appellation. (654 Kendall Road; open daily from 11 am to 5 pm; 800-84FORIS; *www.foriswine.com*.)

Leaving Foris, turn right onto the Loop Road, then left at the dead end (46) to return to Cave Junction, unless you will be visiting the caves, in which case you'd turn right at the dead end. When your travels are over, retrace your steps (46 to 199 to 238 to 99) to return to Ashland.

ROGUE-UMPQUA SCENIC DRIVE

Just when you thought you knew southern Oregon, you get a glimpse of the wonders along this route and realize your vision was far too limited. Start in Ashland and take I-5 North to 234 east, toward and through the friendly town of **Gold Hill**. (A quicker route to Crater Lake would involve getting off I-5 about 15 miles sooner and following 62 North, which we'll soon join a little less directly.) Enjoy this lush valley byway to Hwy 62 and then head north. You'll pass through small towns like **Shady Cove**, which attracts anglers and river rafters from all over the area, through two state parks (**Casey** and **Joseph Stewart**), drive past the town of **Prospect**, and up to historic **Union Creek**. Stop when you see signs near Union Creek to the **Rogue Gorge and Natural Bridge Interpretive Center** so you can marvel at the river as it thunders through deep and narrow chasms here.

To bypass Crater Lake altogether, which may be necessary depending on time and the weather, take Hwy 230 just north of Union Creek. From this stretch you'll still have an impressive view of the peaks and ridges that remain of Mount Mazama following its eruption more than 7,500 years ago. Watch for signs to the **Crater Rim Viewpoint**. Take 230 to Hwy 138 in the direction of Diamond Lake. If you are taking this route, skip now to the final three paragraphs in this itinerary. Otherwise, we'll take you now to Crater Lake.

Whether you want only a glimpse or a full day at **Crater Lake National Park**, you'll enter from the southern entrance off 62 (follow the signs from Union Creek). At 1,932 feet, Crater Lake is the deepest lake in the U.S., which accounts for the intensity of its vibrant blue color. Only six other lakes in the entire world are any deeper than this! The lake resides inside the caldera of a collapsed volcano called Mount Mazama. It is encircled by mountains that stay blanketed in snow nearly all year and makes for a truly memorable visit at the right time of year (usually July through September). There is a weekly per-car admission charge.

Crater Lake

Our first stop is the **Steel Information Center**, open at all times of the year. It's a humble setup but a good place to get oriented. Enter the park from Hwy 62 and turn left where the road dead ends to head north, following the signs to the Information Center. An 18-minute video will introduce you to the Crater Lake story. Pick up a detailed area map only if you're going to spend the day in the park; otherwise we'll guide you. (Open daily from 9 am to 5 pm; 541-594-2211.)

Head north again on **Rim Drive**. In its entirety, Rim Drive (open July to mid-October) is 33 miles long and steers you along the edge of this awe-inspiring caldera. Without stops it would take you about two hours to complete, but we're going to recommend some spectacular trails (choosing only the easiest), viewpoints, and branch roads along the way, so that you can really appreciate where you are. And don't worry: we'll tell you where to exit if you're here only for a quick visit.

These stopovers appear in order as you take Rim Drive in a clockwise direction from the Steel Information Center:

The **Sinnott Memorial Overlook** (in Rim Village on the south side of the lake and open in summer only) is your first chance to see this beautiful lake. Rangers offer excellent lectures here. A 100-foot paved path leads to unimpeded views in all directions.

The Watchman offers one of the most breathtaking views on the entire drive (good news for those moving on soon). It's also the closest view you'll get of Wizard Island, which formed after the initial collapse of the volcano more than 7,500 years ago. Consider taking the hike to the site of a former fire tower (almost 1½ miles round trip). The view from there is amazing.

For the visitor ready to leave the park now, it's shortly after The Watchman that you'll exit in the direction of Diamond Lake on Hwy 138. These travelers should skip now to the final three paragraphs of this itinerary. Otherwise, continue along Rim Drive to linger at these additional spots:

Cloudcap (a 1-mile spur road west of Rim Drive) is the highest point accessible by car. You'll have nearly an aerial view of the lake from this vantage, as well as a 360-degree view of the superb surroundings: dense forests, the Klamath Basin with its own lake, and Mount Scott, which at 8,926 feet is the highest peak in the park.

Phantom Ship (you will view it from Kerr Notch where Rim Road meets Pinnacles Road) offers a glimpse at a 300-foot-long island (actually an exposed section of lava dike) rising out of the lake, which may remind you of a sailing ship. Hikers can get a closer look via a half-mile round-trip trail.

The Pinnacles (accessed via a 7-mile spur road southeast of Rim Drive at Kerr Notch) takes you a distance away from the lake to witness a piece of volcanic mystery. Here, hundreds of hollow spires, made of pumice and scoria (volcanic ash) and called fumaroles, show the effect of years of erosion. Some fumaroles rise eerily as many as 80 feet above the ground. Signage will describe the fascinating details of their formation.

Return to Rim Drive and if you've had enough, take 62 back out of the park all the way to I-5 heading south back to Ashland. Otherwise, continue on Rim Drive until you see the next set of signs for exiting the park (just past The Watchman in the direction of Diamond Lake on Hwy 138).

Certainly you might consider booking a room at the **Crater Lake Lodge** in Rim Village. While the lodge is not among our recommendations for best places to stay, it is convenient. Reservations are best made well in advance by calling 541-830-8700 Monday to Friday from 8 am to 4 pm. The lodge is open in summer months only.

Continue our Rogue-Umpqua loop excursion by taking Hwy 138 through the resort community of **Diamond Lake**, nestled between Mount Bailey and Mount Thielsen, and on into the thick of the gorgeous **Umpqua National Forest**. This part of the state is legendary for fly-fishing for steelhead trout, whitewater rafting, kayaking, and many other recreational pursuits. It's a wild and verdant area that passes dramatic rock outcroppings (**Old Man Rock** and **Eagle Creek**) as well as the beautiful **Toketee Reservoir** and **Swiftwater Park**.

If you have the time, don't miss an opportunity to pull over and enjoy at least one of the many well marked trails, including **Susan Creek Falls**, **Toketee Falls**, or **Watson Falls**. See our listing for the **Steamboat Inn** for one of our favorite recommendations. It's a perfect choice for overnighting in this area so that you can really enjoy its rich magnificence—at least try to have a meal there. In the community of **Glide**, stop at **Colliding Rivers** to admire the spot where the North Umpqua and the Little River converge.

Carry on to the town of Roseburg, then take a beautiful stretch of I-5 southward back to Ashland, or to one of our recommended inns in Jacksonville or Merlin.

Leadbetter Pt SP.
Oysterville
Fort Canby SP
Ilwaco
Warrenton
Seaside
Ecola SP
Cannon Beach
Manzanita
Manhatan Beach SP
Oceanside
Netarts
Pacific City
Neskowin
Lincoln City
Depoe Bay
Newport
Yaquina Head
Waldport

WA

Columbia R.

Astoria
Fort Clatsop NM
Oswald SP
McMinnville

Tillamook

Sandlake

Otis

OR

Salem

Willamette River

Portland

Eugene

Cape Perpetua
Florence
Reedsport
Oregon
Dunes NRA
North Bend
Coos Bay   Cape Arago SP
Charleston
Bullards Beach SP
Bandon

Port Orford

Gold Beach

Brookings

Umpqua River

Rogue River
Merlin
Galice
Grants Pass
Rogue River

Boardman SP
Azalea SP
Loeb SP
Harbor

**Edge of
the World**

● Orientation/
  Sightseeing

⌇ Itinerary Route

30
26
18
5
20
101
126
23
199

Edge of the World
The Oregon Coast

A trip along the Oregon coast is like a trip along the very edge of the world, where one small piece of North America comes finally to an end and drops dramatically into the Pacific Ocean. Mist and mild temperatures, awe-inspiring scenery, and a wide range of recreational activities make this one of the state's most popular regions for Oregonians and visitors alike. Here one comes to revel in quiet; in raw and rugged landscapes and unspoiled sandy beaches; in revitalizing ocean breezes; and for the liberating sensation of sheer space and remoteness. Town populations are small. The way of life is relaxed and unhurried. When deciding how you want to approach your visit, keep in mind that it is not at all necessary to make the entire 362-mile trip from the California to the Washington border (or vice versa, of course) to appreciate the beauty and wonder of the coastline. One- and two-day trips from many of the destinations we cover in other Oregon itineraries are not only realistic, but a great way to mix things up a bit and enjoy a variety of the landscapes that make the state so unique. The approach we'll take here is to segment the coast into three separate sections: South Coast, Central Coast, and North Coast. We'll highlight our favorite spots along the way and interject an alternative route or two to inland places of interest in case you do decide to mix and match itineraries to vary your experience.

Recommended Pacing: If you want to take a top-to-bottom approach and focus all your attention on the ocean setting, you might spend two nights in each of the three regions we cover here. If you are combining your visit with other inland regions of the state, remember that day trips are easy. You can get to the north coast from Portland in about an hour. We once made a perfect day trip from Portland, taking Hwy 18 westward through the Willamette Valley, heading up the coast as far as Cannon Beach, then back to the city via Hwy 26. We had plenty of time to make spontaneous stops along the way, including a delicious waterfront dinner in Cannon Beach. Likewise, the central coast is a stone's throw from Eugene, and the south coast makes a great sojourn from the Ashland area.

SOUTH COAST

California's densest redwood forests greet the state of Oregon here, where the rugged Siskiyou Mountains give way to a series of rocky headlands and the mighty Rogue River cuts a path to the Pacific. Coastal rainforests on the south coast are considered among the most diverse in the country.

Let's take 101 North from the California border to our first stop in **Brookings**. This particular segment of coastline enjoys the warmest coastal weather in the entire Pacific Northwest. Flowers thrive here, especially Easter lilies and other varieties known to prefer winter months. You might take a stroll through **Azalea Park** (watch for signs off 101 just west of the Chetco River Bridge) to enjoy a display of some the area's most prized blooms. In April and May the azaleas are at their most glorious, but you can count on a beautiful display no matter what the time of year.

We took a short, easy walk through nearby **Loeb State Park** (farther inland via the same road that took us to Azalea Park; open daily year round; 541-469-2021). With a printed handout we collected at the **Redwood Grove Nature Trail** trailhead, we learned how to tell the difference between a coastal redwood and a Douglas fir, the difference between four varieties of ferns, and what to call that gold-bellied creature that kept skittering across our path: a newt! It is a tranquil thing indeed to walk through a forest like this.

Boardman State Park is only 4 miles north of downtown Brookings. (Open year round from dawn to dusk; 800-551-6949.) This is an absolutely gorgeous stretch of coastline, providing multiple opportunities to pull over and draw inspiration from the beauty of your surroundings. Two stops in particular are simply required now that you're here: the trail to the **Thomas Creek Bridge** and the brief walk to **Natural Bridge Cove**. Both are located very near the north end of the park. Watch for signs.

It's at **Gold Beach** that the powerful **Rogue River** empties into the Pacific Ocean. Whatever else you decide to do in this area, don't miss the chance to sign up for a jet-boat excursion up the mighty Rogue. Some 40 miles of riverside from Gold Beach to Grants Pass are protected within the **Siskiyou National Forest**, where the only access is by foot or boat, so this is a perfect opportunity for an intimate glimpse into this beautiful wild place. We recommend **Jerry's Rogue River Jet Boats** for an entertaining, educational, and invigorating adventure (May through October, 800-451-3645, *www.roguejets.com.*) Boats depart from a well marked dock located in Gold Beach on the south side of the bridge that crosses the Rogue as you travel north on 101. These trips are perfect for all ages, so if you're traveling with children, consider this a terrific way to spend the day. Jerry's vessels are modern riverboats custom designed for the river and certified by the Coast Guard, so you don't have to worry about safety. Tours of different lengths are available, but we encourage you to take the 104-mile excursion to venture deep into the forest and climb some 350 feet up a series of rapids. Allow eight hours for a round trip, which includes lunch or dinner, depending on your departure time. The first leg of the journey takes place in a lovely estuary where temperatures are often chilly, so grab one of the on-board blankets—you won't need it long as you make your way east into the hotter, drier inland areas. Your guide will describe the gorgeous surroundings and you'll have fun looking for river otters, birds, deer, and even bears. At the rustic and forested town of **Agness**, you'll switch to a smaller boat, one better designed to navigate the narrow gorges, hairpin turns, and shallow rapids ahead. This is truly a voyage now! At **Paradise Lodge** farther inland, you'll stop for sustenance before making your reluctant way back to the ocean. Talk to Jerry about the option to spend the night at Paradise Lodge, if you prefer. Guestrooms are small and plainly furnished, but appropriate to this spot so far from civilization!

Alternative Inland Loop: Southern Oregon (well, *all* of Oregon, for that matter) is replete with scenic back roads providing alternative ways to get around. From June to about early October—when snowfall doesn't close it—the **Shasta Costa Road** from Gold Beach to **Galice** is a great adventure: an intimate look at the sylvan Siskiyou National Forest on an only-recently, sometimes-questionably, paved and narrow road that proves a rewarding break from the "usual." If you have the time to move slowly, try this route. Watch for signs from just north of Gold Beach on 101 directing you east toward Agness or Galice (the Shasta Costa Road is also called 33, and later 23). You'll feel far removed from civilization as you make your way through the forest. From Galice, follow signs to the tiny hamlet of **Merlin** (there's a great inn in this unlikeliest of places; see the **Pine Meadow Inn**) and on to Grants Pass. Your loop might take you south from Grants Pass on 199 South through the Kalmiopsis Wilderness, on through the immense, redwood groves and impossible, rock-bound canyons of the **Smith River Gorge**, all the way back to Hwy 101 near Crescent City. From here, it's a quick trip (about 40 miles) back up to Gold Beach. Refer to our **Southern Oregon itinerary** for a look at all there is to do inland in this beautiful region.

Coquille River Lighthouse

From Gold Beach, continue on 101 North to **Bandon**. Exit at either Chicago, 2nd, or Delaware Streets and follow the signs to **Old Town**. Visitors enjoy rambling through Old Town to enjoy the shops and fine galleries or to watch the fishing boats sail in and out of the harbor. But nature is what really calls to you in this corner of the world. At the west end of 11th Street, for example, right off Beach Loop Drive, you'll find **Coquille Point**. Take a walk on the paved trail there and enjoy views of beautiful **Bandon Beach** with its strange sea stacks and profusion of birds. Two miles north of Bandon on 101, a gentle 3-mile road through **Bullards Beach State Park** (open daily year round; 541-347-2209) guides you through coastal forest, along the north bank of the Coquille Estuary, and out to the **Coquille River Lighthouse**, one of nine stately lighthouses to stand guard along the Oregon coastline.

The old lumber towns of **Coos Bay**, **North Bend**, and **Charleston** are sometimes referred to as Oregon's "Bay Area," once an extremely busy commercial hub where the timber industry thrived. Today, visitors arc drawn here by three landmarks immediately southwest of Coos Bay via the Cape Arago midway: Shore Acres State Park, Cape Arago State Park, and South Slough National Estuarine Preserve. (Look for signs to the midway between Bandon and Coos Bay on 101.) Once the grounds of a 20th-century private estate, **Shore Acres** is now an impressive 743-acre garden, the winner of numerous landscape design awards, and most notable for its many unusual botanicals. (Open year round daily from 8 am to dusk.) At nearby **Cape Arago State Park**, an easy trail leads north along a ridge to an excellent vantage point for viewing the marine animals that make these offshore rocks their home. On clear days, you can see south to Bandon, but in a winter storm, watch out! Winds can reach epic proportions on this ridge. (Open year round, daily, from 8 am to dusk; 541-888-3778 or 800-551-6949.) You might also enjoy a visit to **South Slough National Estuarine Preserve**, one of seven tidal inlets that collectively form the Coos Estuary. An **Interpretive Center** is open to the public (daily from Memorial Day to Labor Day, from 8 am to 4 pm; 541-888-5558). It houses exhibits, a video viewing area, and a bookstore, and there is an outdoor amphitheater for special presentations (or just for resting). Several easy trails, varying in length from ¼ mile to 3 miles, give you immediate access to this preserve, which is peaceful yet teeming with life. Try the wonderful **Estuary Study Trail**, a 3-mile series of scenic loops.

CENTRAL COAST

Stretching some 40 miles from Coos Bay to Florence, the **Oregon Dunes National Recreation Area** is considered one of the best examples of coastal dune formation anywhere in the country. Roughly midway, some 11 miles south of Reedsport on the ocean side of 101, watch for signs to the **Umpqua Scenic Dunes Trail**. Park the car, take off your shoes, and get out on the open sand! Farther up the road, about 10 miles south of Florence, three raised platforms provide excellent viewpoints, informative signage, and an easy 1-mile trail across the dunes to the beach.

The **Cape Perpetua Scenic Area** just south of Yachats (say YAH hots) has to be one of the most beautiful sections of the Oregon coast. Characterized by 2,700 acres of Sitka spruce rainforest, it's a Sherwood Forest right out of your dreams. Stop at the **Interpretive Center** right off 101 to see films and exhibits about the area. (Open daily between Memorial Day and Labor Day from 9 am to 5 pm, and 10 am to 4 pm on weekends the rest of the year; 541-547-3289.) While you're at it, collect walking maps, for there are some 23 miles of stunning trails in this region. Try the half-mile **Captain Cook Trail**, taking you from forest to ancient basalt at the water's edge.

Next stop, **Newport**, established in 1882, and today a bustling coastal community of over 9,000 people. Its heart is a working waterfront on Yaquina Bay, where fishing fleets and fresh seafood markets share space with galleries, shops, and restaurants. You'll want to visit Newport's first-class **Oregon Coast Aquarium**, where five impressive indoor exhibits offer intimate views of life on the Oregon shoreline and out in the open sea. The *Passages of the Deep* exhibit is really something: you'll feel like an underwater explorer as you come face to face with sharks, rockfish, and sting rays from an underwater tunnel. Be sure to see the *Enchanted Seas* exhibit, which takes you on a journey into the mystical world of seahorses, sea dragons, and other magical sea creatures. Six acres of outdoor exhibits add to this comprehensive sea museum, including your chance to get up-close peeks at sea otters, harbor seals, sea lions, tufted puffins, a giant Pacific octopus, and a walk-through seabird aviary. (2820 SE Ferry Slip Road; open daily Memorial Day to Labor Day, from 9 am to 6 pm, and after Labor Day, from 10 am to 5 pm; 541-867-3474; *www.aquarium.org*.)

Four miles north of Newport, the **Interpretive Center** at **Yaquina Head Outstanding Natural Area** (follow the signage off Hwy 101) offers first-rate exhibits and videos to introduce you to this unique spot: a 100-acre column of ancient lava stretching 1 mile out into the ocean. (Open daily, year round; 541-574-3100.) Just south of the center, at the tip of the Quarry Cove Inter-tidal headlands, stands **Yaquina Lighthouse** (open daily from June 15th to September 15th for guided morning tours, weather permitting), built in 1873 and billed as the tallest lighthouse on the Oregon coast at 93 feet.

NORTH COAST

Let's leave Hwy 101 for a moment and get a break from the highway. About 30 miles north of Newport, take a right onto Hwy 18. Stop at the **Otis Café** in **Otis** (just a couple of miles up Hwy 18 on your left) for an amazing piece of fresh-from-the-oven fruit pie. It's a down-home, Northwest roadside café that locals love. Order that pie à la mode! (Open every day in summer from 7 am to 9 pm. When the "kids are back in school," hours change: Monday to Thursday from 7 am to 3 pm, and from 7 am to 9 pm on Friday, Saturday, and Sunday.) As you leave the café, head north on **Old Scenic Highway 101** (it's well marked alongside the café) and take it a brief, but lovely, distance as it wends through quiet sections of the Suislaw National Forest and returns you to 101 at Neskowin.

> **Alternative Inland Loop from Portland**: If you are exploring the North Coast by way of the Portland area, a great loop might look something like this: Starting in Portland, take I-5 South to 99W (the "Wine Road") through the Willamette Valley. Pick up Hwy 18 in McMinnville and follow it out to the coast. Head north on 101, following the route recommended in the North Coast portion of this itinerary, then head east again at Cannon Beach on Hwy 26, for a sylvan path back to the city. Depending on how much you want to see and do as you go, you can either make this a long but fulfilling day trip, or extend the journey by spending the night on the coast before returning to the city. See the **Portland Area** itinerary, especially the **Wine Country** section, for ideas on fun things to do en route to the coast.

About 7 miles north of **Neskowin**, you'll have another chance to turn off the highway and get closer to the water. Taking these scenic detours is the best way to enjoy the coast, time permitting, since many stretches of 101 pass through some less-than-appealing settings. Turn left onto Brooten Road to follow the signs for **3 Capes Scenic Route**, a 39-mile detour along the water, through forests, and past the remote seaside communities of **Pacific City**, **Sandlake**, **Netarts**, and **Oceanside**. (You'll have several opportunities to cut back to 101 as you go, in case you find yourself pressed for time.) A couple of miles past Pacific City, the coast unfolds dramatically as rolling, forested hills spill into the ocean. Take advantage of turnouts and viewpoints when you can. If you have time for a walk, we recommend the **Cape Lookout Trailhead** (about 2–3 miles *before* reaching Cape Lookout State Park), from which you'll have your choice of three routes, ranging from 1-4/5 to 2-2/5 miles and from easy to difficult, through coastal rainforests and along rocky cliffs. Breathtaking views!

The 3 Capes Scenic Route will join 101 again near **Tillamook**, the center of Oregon's dairy industry. You might want to stop here and visit the **Pioneer Museum** (2106 Second St; open Monday to Saturday from 8 am to 5 pm, Sunday from 11 am to 5 pm; 503-842-4553) or drive 2 miles south of town to the **Tillamook Air Museum**, an impressive private collection of World War II aircraft (6030 Hangar Road; open daily from 10 am to 5 pm; 503-842-1130). On your way north on the 101, you can watch cheese being made at the **Tillamook Cheese Factory**, just outside town (4175 Hwy 101 N; open daily from 8 am to 8 pm, June 15 to September 15; from 8 am to 6 pm the rest of the year; 503-815-1300). A few miles south of Nehalem, **Manhattan Beach** is wide and sandy, good for strolling and soaking in the sun (follow the signs off 101 to **Manhattan Beach State Wayside** and walk the short path to the beach). The town of **Manzanita** is funky and friendly, with great beaches and enviable ocean-view homes in the hills. The next stretch of 101 North from Manzanita is just beautiful. You'll pass the verdant **Oswald West State Park**, a popular spot for camping and fishing (503-368-3575), and the tiny romantic beach at **Hug Point**.

The next village of **Cannon Beach** is considered the center for artistic activity on the Oregon coast. It is more contemporary and more sophisticated, especially along **Hemlock Street**, than many of its counterpart coastal towns, all the while retaining a small-town feeling. Travelers come to enjoy the shops and restaurants, but no visit here would be complete without a stop at the pristine and magnificent **Ecola State Park** (open from 6 am to 10 pm daily year round; 503-436-2844). Ecola ("Whale Creek" to the native Indians) was the spot at which William Clark, Sacajawea, and the men of the Corps of Discovery traded with Tillamook Indians in 1806 for whale blubber and whale meat, in a no-doubt deliriously happy transaction to supplement their spartan and monotonous diets. So taken was Clark with this particular stretch of coastline, that an awestruck description appears in his journal. This 1,300-acre park includes a picture-perfect stretch of beach that's great for walking. A waterside forest of old-growth Sitka spruce and western hemlock makes for a protected habitat for elk and deer. For a good 6-mile hike, try the **Tillamook Head Trail** beginning at Indian Beach. Prefer a short stroll to an amazing overlook? Try **Ecola Point** just 2 miles north of the park entrance, where a ¼-mile path leads you from the parking lot to the headlands.

Speaking of Lewis and Clark, the **Fort Clatsop National Memorial**, where a 125-acre site honors the 1805–06 winter encampment of the expedition, is a must-see for those interested in this remarkable piece of American history (follow signs to Fort Clatsop Road off Business 101; open daily from 8 am to 5 pm). A community-built replica of the explorers' fort is the focus. A large **Visitor Center** includes two theaters and an excellent exhibit hall. (Hours vary seasonally; 503-861-2471.)

At the very top of the Oregon coast sits the oldest American settlement west of the Rockies, **Astoria**. It was first visited by the English Captain Robert Gray in 1792, then by the Lewis and Clark Expedition in 1805, and thereafter by adventurous pioneers by the thousands. Today a great many restored buildings keep that history alive.

Founded in 1962, the **Columbia River Maritime Museum** is home to one of the nation's finest displays of model ships and nautical relics. In a 37,000-square-foot space, the museum presents more than 7,000 artifacts, plus the lightship *Columbia*, a National Historic Landmark. (1792 Marine Drive on the waterfront; open daily from 9:30 am to 5 pm; 503-325-2323; *www.crmm.org*.)

Climb the 125-foot-high **Astoria Column**, patterned after Trajan's Column in Rome. The mural art that makes up the exterior of the column is truly impressive, depicting the westward expansion of settlers into the area and Oregon's early history. From the top of the column, you'll have an excellent view of the Pacific Ocean, the Columbia River,

Saddle Mountain, and the Clatsop Plain. (From downtown, drive uphill on 16th Street and follow the signage. It's open from 7 am to dusk every day.)

Astoria celebrates its Scandinavian heritage with the **Scandinavian Midsummer Festival**, held every year in mid-June. This is when local Icelanders, Finns, Danes, Norwegians, and Swedes gather to celebrate their cultures with pole dancing, bonfires that destroy evil spirits, authentic Scandinavian music, a smorgasbord of old-world delicacies, crafts, and a parade.

Alternative Side Trip: True Lewis and Clark enthusiasts would do well to make the trip across the Astoria Bridge over to the Long Beach Peninsula in Washington to see **Fort Canby State Park**—see the following section.

Also of special interest, The Lewis & Clark Explorer Train: The Lewis & Clark Explorer Train travels from Portland along the Oregon side of the lower Columbia River to Astoria. The train takes you close to several historic sites and through the countryside visited and traversed by the famous Lewis & Clark Corps of Discovery Expedition. Train schedules are seasonal. (*www.lcbo.net/train.html*)

LONG BEACH PENINSULA

If you've come this far, you might be interested in pushing on a bit farther in a trip to Washington State's **Long Beach Peninsula**, a long (28 miles) spit of land that separates Willapa Bay from the Pacific Ocean. It's a quiet spot, long ago inhabited by the Chinook Indians, with a surprising selection of unique inns and the promise of tranquility. A glimpse of Northwest history, fishing, and strolling wild and sandy beaches: these pleasures have lured visitors to this corner of Washington State for years.

Fort Canby State Park resides at the southernmost tip of the peninsula. It's primarily a camping and picnicking spot, but Lewis and Clark historians will appreciate the **Lewis and Clark Interpretive Center** there (open daily from 10 am to 5 pm; 360-642-3029). Perched high on a cliff overlooking **Cape Disappointment**, the center reminds us that it was here that the Corps of Discovery first reached the shores of the Pacific. Before jetties were constructed to control its sandbar, the mouth of the Columbia was known as the "Graveyard of the Pacific." You'll take a self-guided tour detailing the events of the momentous Lewis and Clark Expedition and follow a path to the **Cape Disappointment Lighthouse**, the oldest (1856) operating lighthouse on the West Coast. A tour of nearby **North Head Lighthouse**, perched atop layers of pillow basalt (formations that shape when lava hits the ocean) is available daily from 10 am to 6 pm between April and October (360-642-3078).

Protected by tall headlands to the west, **Ilwaco** lies just northeast of Cape Disappointment. It's a popular spot for sports fishermen and a wonderful place to stay.

Oysterville at the northern end of the peninsula was, in the 19th century, a key supplier of oysters to the city of San Francisco. The town is now on the National Register of Historic Places. Buildings of note include a church, an oyster cannery, and an old post office. The peninsula is still a great place for sampling the oysters of Willapa Bay.

Leadbetter Point State Park, at the very top of the peninsula, offers hiking trails through coastal forest, across sand dunes, and over mudflats to the beach or bay. (Open daily year round from dawn to dusk; 360-642-3078.)

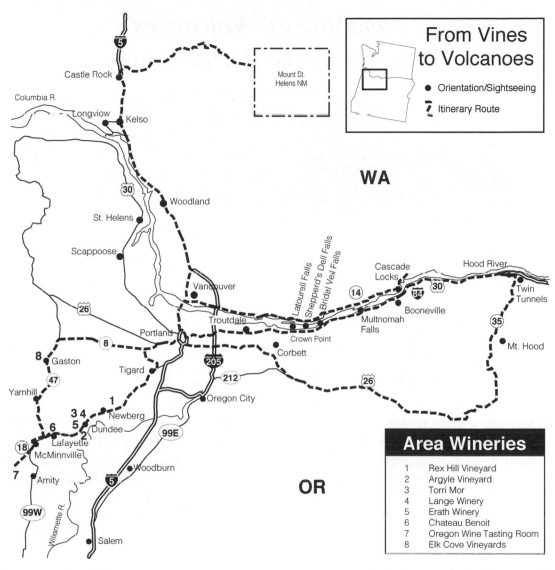

From Vines to Volcanoes

Mount St. Helens NM

- Orientation/Sightseeing
- Itinerary Route

WA

OR

Castle Rock
Columbia R.
Longview
Kelso
Woodland
St. Helens
Scappoose
Vancouver
Troutdale
Portland
Gaston
Tigard
Yamhill
Newberg
Dundee
Lafayette
McMinnville
Amity
Woodburn
Salem
Oregon City
Corbett
Crown Point
Latourell Falls
Shepperd's Dell Falls
Bridal Veil Falls
Multnomah Falls
Cascade Locks
Booneville
Hood River
Twin Tunnels
Mt. Hood

Area Wineries

1 Rex Hill Vineyard
2 Argyle Vineyard
3 Torri Mor
4 Lange Winery
5 Erath Winery
6 Chateau Benoit
7 Oregon Wine Tasting Room
8 Elk Cove Vineyards

From Vines to Volcanoes
Discovering the Portland Area

Willamette Valley

Where the Willamette River joins the mighty Columbia and the two head out together in search of the Pacific Ocean, the quietly sophisticated city of Portland flourishes. Ideally located for enjoying some of the Pacific Northwest's most remarkable natural and historic wonders, Portland is less than 80 miles east of the Pacific Ocean, only 65 miles south of Mount St. Helens National Volcanic Monument, 16 miles west of the arresting beauty of the Columbia River Gorge, minutes away from the heart of the wine country, and about 110 miles from Fort Clatsop National Memorial, where Meriwether Lewis and

William Clark spent their first west coast winter in 1805–06. This itinerary introduces you to the many attractions that the city has to offer, then guides you on round trips through lovely countryside to explore the flourishing Yamhill County wine region, the scenic Columbia River Highway and Mount Hood, and the awesome Mount St. Helens.

Recommended Pacing: Plan to spend at least two days and three nights in Portland itself, depending on what you are interested in seeing. We recommend taking at least two (or a luxurious three) days to enjoy the Yamhill County wine country. There are wonderful inns in the area and the surroundings are so lovely; it would be a shame to rush your way through it. If one day is absolutely all you have time for, follow the itinerary through to a visit to Erath Vineyards Winery—as much for the fun of the roads themselves as for the great tastings—then head back to Portland. For the Columbia River and Mount Hood, a minimum of two days and one overnight would enable you to enjoy this scenic loop. However, if a day trip from Portland is all you have time for, concentrate your time in the gorge area, following this itinerary only as far as Cascade Locks and heading back to Portland along the other side of the river. For Mount St. Helens, allow one full day from Portland and back (an eight-hour trip allowed us plenty of time for leisurely visits to three of the visitor centers, plus a stop for lunch at Hoffstadt Bluffs).

PORTLAND

Portland is a very easy city to get around in. There are many inexpensive parking lots in the downtown area, so park your car and venture out on foot. Maps and self-guided tours are available at the **Visitor Information and Services Center** located in the **Pioneer Courthouse Square** complex. (701 SW Sixth Ave. Suite 1; open weekdays from 8:30 am to 5:30 pm, and Saturday from 10 am to 4 pm; 503-275-8355, *www.pova.com.*) When visiting neighborhoods, you can drive, park, walk, or consider public transportation. A good bus (Tri-Met), light-rail (MAX), and a vintage trolley system work in tandem so that you can use tickets interchangeably, and it's free in the downtown area.

This is a city that goes to great lengths to ensure that nature plays an active part in daily life. Over 200 parks grace the city and an ordinance prohibiting the construction of buildings higher than 40 stories guarantees that the Cascade and Coastal mountain ranges are never obscured by "progress." Take a drive up to **Council Crest Park** set over 1,000 feet above the city and accessed via Fairmount Blvd, it's a wonderful spot for viewing all five Cascade peaks—weather permitting, of course.

No self-respecting lover of books would consider missing a turn of several hours at **Powell's City of Books**, 1005 W. Burnside Street. It takes up an entire city block (in a building that once served as a used-car dealership and car repair shop) and holds a computerized inventory of over one million titles—the largest used and new book selection under one roof in the world. Color-coded maps are available at the front desk for making your way through literally thousands of sections. The *Seattle Times* has aptly called Powell's "a place of staggering ambition, hidden in the very humble wrapper of a worn-out warehouse." (Open from 9 am to 11 pm every day; 503-228-0540 or 866-201-7601, *www.powells.com*.)

Take a self-guided tour through the *Portland!* exhibit at the **Oregon History Center** located at 1200 SW Park Avenue. It's a marvelous orientation to the area's history, beginning with the 1840s when the first European and American settlers arrived, and continuing to the present day. Notice the "copper" displayed at the exhibit entrance. It was used in the now-famous coin toss of 1845, by which city builders Asa Lovejoy of Boston, Massachusetts and Francis Pettygrove of Portland, Maine decided the name of their new city! (Open Tuesday to Saturday from 10 am to 5 pm; till 8 pm on Thursday; and Sunday from noon to 5 pm; 503-222-1741, *www.ohs.org*.)

Art lovers will enjoy the renovated **Portland Art Museum** at 1219 SW Park Avenue. Founded in 1892, the museum has (over many loving years) amassed a diverse collection numbering over 32,000 works of art. A $45-million renovation and construction project resulted in over 50,000 square feet dedicated to the Centers for Native American Art and Northwest Art. Additional renovation projects account for new permanent galleries, a community education center, a new museum shop, and a café. (Open Tuesday to Saturday from 10 am to 5 pm, and Sunday from noon to 5 pm; 503-226-2811; *www.pam.org*.)

Washington Park can easily occupy the better part of a day if you're inclined to enjoy all it has to offer: an arboretum, a zoo, a forestry center, and much, much more. Two gardens in particular make for rejuvenating contemplative strolls. The enchanting **Japanese Garden** (611 SW Kingston Avenue; hours vary; 503-223-1321) occupies nearly 6 undulating acres and provides an authentic look at the genius of Japanese landscape masters. Enjoy the Tea Garden, the Strolling Pond Garden, and the Zen-inspired Sand and Stone Garden. Also worth the time is the **International Rose Test Garden**, where more than 8,000 roses representing hundreds of species grow in terraces overlooking the city and Mount Hood. (400 SW Kingston Avenue; open daily from dawn to dusk; 503-823-3636.)

Downtown Portland

One of our favorite picnic/viewing spots is the lawn area in front of **Pittock Mansion** (head west up Burnside, turn right on NW Barnes, then follow the signs). Completed in 1914, this fine home was built for Henry Pittock who came west on the Oregon Trail in 1853. Pittock made his fortune through a variety of wise and timely investments and became publisher of the *Oregonian*. On a good day, the views of Mount Hood and the city from this spot are wonderful. Tours of the mansion are available daily from 11 am to 4 pm but the grounds are free to stroll while the sun is up (503-823-3624).

The **Portland Classical Chinese Garden** (also called the Garden of Awakening Orchids) occupies an entire city block between NW Third Avenue and NW Everett Street. It's a unique urban garden patterned in a 15th-century Ming style and designed by architects and artisans from the Chinese city of Suzhou. Created to inspire residents living in busy cities, Chinese gardens were meant to offer respite in the center of activity. Today's visitors to this setting will find a garden little changed from what would have greeted them more than 500 years ago in dynastic China. (Open November through March from 10 am to 5 pm and from April through October from 9 am to 6 pm.)

For over one hundred years the city has adopted the rose as a symbol of its continuing growth and renewal. If you're visiting in June, find a schedule of **Rose Festival** activities, which start with the coronation of the Rose Festival Queen on or around May 31st. Fireworks, parades, boat races, musical performances, and special art exhibits make for a month-long celebration of the city's favorite time of year.

Want to tour Oregon wineries without leaving downtown? Then the place to go is **Oregon Wines on Broadway** at 515 SW Broadway. It's a charming wine bar where you can sample two dozen or more of the state's finest wines. (Closed Mondays, but usually open into the evening hours on other days.)

Beer aficionados may want to find out how Portland got its title of "Microbrewery Capital of the World." On Saturday afternoons, **Brewbus** offers a four-hour, behind-the-scenes tour of various breweries in town (*www.brewbus.com*).

Governor Tom McCall Waterfront Park gives you the chance to stroll alongside the Willamette River for an easy mile and a half, with a view of eight Portland bridges if you walk from one end to the other. This park is often the venue for summertime concerts.

Reserve a spot on a **Portland Spirit River Cruise** from the Salmon Street Springs dock along the waterfront walk. It's a fun, two-hour cruise on a 150-foot yacht. You'll sail up the Willamette and past Ross Island, home to bald eagles, great blue herons, ospreys, and private riverside estates. Choose from sightseeing rides as well as lunch and dinner cruises. (503-224-3900 or 800-224-3901.)

The **Pearl District**, bounded by W Burnside, NW Lovejoy, NW 8th Avenue, and NW 15th Avenue, is getting a great deal of attention these days. Formerly an industrial area, it has been transformed in the last ten years into a popular spot for upscale lofts, art galleries, boutique shops, great restaurants, and sidewalk cafés. The neighboring **Nob Hill District**, bordered by NW 15th Avenue, NW 23rd Avenue, W Burnside, and NW Lovejoy, is absolutely charming, especially for its mid-19th-century homes. Wander in and among these neighborhood streets, pausing when something takes your fancy. Make your way down NW 23rd and NW 21st Streets.

Forest Park offers some 50 miles of interconnected trails that wind up and down the slopes of this 5,000-acre wonderland, the largest urban park in North America. Maps are available to give you options. The Wildwood Trail extends for 33 miles from Forest Park to Washington Park.

The **Oregon Museum of Science and Industry** at 1945 SE Water Street offers excellent exhibits in a contemporary building right on the Willamette River. It features the Murdock Planetarium, an Omnimax Theater, and tours of the submarine used in the movie *The Hunt for Red October*. (Open from 9:30 am to 7 pm, daily, mid-June to Labor Day; and from 9:30 am to 5:30 pm, Tuesday to Sunday the rest of the year; 503-797-4000.)

YAMHILL COUNTY WINE TOUR

Note: If you plan to sample the wines of the Willamette Valley along this route, please select or hire a designated driver.

Running from Oregon's northern border at the Columbia River to the Calapooya Mountains just south of Eugene, the **Willamette Valley** in its entirety is about 200 miles long and 60 miles wide. Sheltered between the Coast Range Mountains to the west and the Cascade Mountains to the east, it is a rich patchwork of prairies, grasslands, forests, orchards, and vineyards. Here the growing season is long and the harvest late (end of September, early October), both conditions serving to intensify the varietal flavors of the grapes. Nearly two-thirds of Oregon's wineries reside in the upper half of the Willamette Valley just southwest of Portland in **Yamhill County**. Known as the "heart of the wine country," this area is blessed with three chains of interlocking hills, all created by millions of years of volcanic activity. It is on the southern and southwestern slopes of these hills that most of the vineyards are planted—ideal spots for grape growing and for Pinot Noirs in particular. Yamhill County is home to dozens of marvelous tasting rooms set in gorgeously picturesque landscapes. We'll take you to some of the best.

From Portland, take I-5 South/Salem to Hwy 99W/Tigard/Newberg (Exit 294). Standard blue winery signs all along Hwy 99W ("The Wine Road") will help you anticipate turns into the vineyards you want to see. Call ahead to confirm hours of operation.

Don't despair at the sight of so many strip malls along the first portion of The Wine Road. We'll get you out of them! About 13 miles after you exit I-5, just north of **Newberg**'s town center and on the right, your first stop is **Rex Hill Vineyard**. Enter a small, elegant building and take your place at an attractive tasting bar. Enjoy the fireplace, the gift shop, the tiny Oregon Wine Brotherhood Museum, or the lovely terraced gardens and picnic area. Established in 1982, Rex Hill is known first for its Pinot Noirs, but also produces top-quality Pinot Gris, Pinot Blanc, Chardonnay, Sauvignon Blanc, and White Riesling. (30835 North Hwy 99W; open from 11 am to 5 pm, daily with extended summer hours; 503-538-0666.) Note: See **Springbrook**

Hazelnut Farm as a recommended place to stay—you can walk through hazelnut orchards to Rex Hill from the inn. Leaving Rex Hill, turn right on Hwy 99W and continue south for about 5 miles to the town of **Dundee**. Stop to visit **Argyle** on your left, which makes its home in a charming, two-story farmhouse built in 1900. Argyle owns 235 acres of prime Willamette Valley vineyard land. It is internationally recognized as a premier producer of New World (*methode champenoise)* sparkling wines; but also produces Chardonnays, Pinot Noirs, and an "old vine" dry Riesling you may want to try. (6901 Hwy 99; open from 11 am to 5 pm, daily; 503-538-8520; *www.argylewinery.com.*)

Right across the street is the handsome **Ponzi Wine Bar**. In addition to featuring the wines of Ponzi Vineyards, the bar presents wines from local producers that don't have tasting rooms and from those in remote areas of the state. You can buy wines by the glass, bottle, or case. Microbrews on draft, Italian coffee, and a selection of cheeses and fresh breads await you, as does a fine selection of wine-themed books. (100 SW 7th Street; open daily from 11 am to 5 pm; 503-554-1500; *www.ponziwines.com.*) The excellent **Dundee Bistro**, also owned by the Ponzi family, is located right next door for those who want a bite to eat.

Leaving Ponzi, continue on 99W and take a right on SW 9th Street and wind your way uphill. Suddenly, the terrain is everything you've been hearing about: the rolling hills, the lovely orchards, rows of vines heavy with fruit. As 9th Street becomes Worden Hill, turn right on Fairview Drive. The road turns to gravel and wends through a forested wilderness to **Torii Mor** on your right. This tasting room is surrounded by a beautiful Japanese garden and boasts stellar views of Olson Vineyard, one of Yamhill County's oldest vineyards. Pinot Noir makes up the bulk of the winery's production, but most are hard-to-come-by reserves and single bottlings. (18325 NE Fairview Drive; open from noon to 5 pm; Saturday and Sunday, February to April; Friday to Sunday, May to November; 800-839-5004; *www.toriimorwinery.com.*)

Leaving Torii Mor, head back to Fairview and turn right out of the drive. Continue past the "Private Road" signage and turn right again at the signs for **Lange Winery**. Enjoy a glass of wine on the back patio, where spectacular views of the Chehalem and Willamette

Valleys will make you forget all your troubles. (18380 NE Buena Vista Drive; open from 11 am to 5 pm, every day except Tuesday; 503-538-6476; *www.langewinery.com*.)

From Lange, turn left onto Fairview to retrace your steps, but only for a few hundred yards, turning right at the first unmarked road (it's actually still Fairview). Drive slowly and enjoy the quiet. Turn left on Worden Hill Road, then right onto the **Erath Vineyards Winery** property, where once again you'll be treated to stunning views in all directions from high in these beautiful Dundee Hills. Wonderful cheeses, crackers, and other fine comestibles are available in the homey tasting room. (9409 NE Worden Hill Road; open from 11 am to 5 pm daily; 503-538-3318 or 800-539-9463; *www.erath.com*.)

Leaving Erath, turn right on Worden Hill, which becomes SW 9th Street. Enjoy the gorgeous orchards and vineyards as you head back to the town of Dundee. Unless you're ready to turn back to Portland, make a right onto Hwy 99W and continue south.

In the town of Lafayette turn right on Mineral Springs Road, following the signs to **Chateau Benoit**. This spectacular hilltop winery is designed like a French chateau and offers panoramic views of Yamhill County. Founded in 1972, it features a crisp Sauvignon Blanc, rich Pinot Noirs, barrel-fermented Chardonnay, and a dry White Riesling, to name but a few. (6580 NE Mineral Springs Road; open from 10 am to 5 pm daily; 503-864-2991; *www.chateaubenoit.com*.)

Leaving Chateau Benoit, turn left to return to 99W and turn right on 99W toward McMinnville. From here, if you've had enough, you can turn right on 47 North to loop back to Portland, or venture bravely past the strip malls and turn left on NE 3rd Street to the historic downtown district of **McMinnville**. The town has two claims to fame: the UFO sighting of May 10, 1950 (stop in at the pub inside McMenamins Hotel to check out the UFO articles) and the **Evergreen Aviation Museum**. Just southeast of McMinnville via 99W South, directly off Hwy 18 (watch for the signs), this aviation museum houses an impressive collection of vintage aircraft. The centerpiece of this collection is the Hughes HK-1 Flying Boat, the **Spruce Goose**, now making its permanent home here. The Spruce Goose, completed in 1947 by famed billionaire/eccentric/aviator Howard Hughes, is the largest airplane ever built, with a wingspan of 320 feet! The entire museum—made largely of glass—was built specifically to house this amazing giant. Also on display beneath the soaring wings of the *Goose* are several fully restored classic airplanes and jets. See a replica of the Wright brothers' 1903 Flyer, several WWII-era fighters and trainers (a P-38 Lightning, a P-51D Mustang, a Supermarine Spitfire, a Messerschmitt Bf 109G-10), as well as Korean War-era jets (a MiG-15 Midget). This museum is a must-see for any aviation buff. (3685 NE Three Mile Lane; open from 9 am to 5 pm, daily except holidays.)

Return to 99W South as you leave the McMinnville area and continue for about 5 miles in the direction of **Amity**. Turn right at Fifth (the Bellevue Highway) then after about 2 miles the road will veer to the right at a sign reading Bellevue/Sheridan. Here's where you have the opportunity to visit a monastery founded by the Swedish Saint Brigit in 1370. It's the only Brigittine (say BRIDGE ih teen) monastery for men left in the world. Guests are welcome, so if you're up for the adventure (and perhaps in the market for some unbelievable homemade fudge), drive straight ahead—rather than veering right— onto Broadmead Road, and continue one additional mile to a sign on your right directing you down a gravel road to the **Brigittine Priory of Our Lady of Consolation**. (If you are not interested in the monastery, just veer right and continue on.) These monks make their own fudge right on these lovely grounds and it's fabulous! Ring the bell, if the door is locked (don't be shy!). One of the monks will greet you, offer you chocolate samples, and direct you to boxes for sale: chocolate cherry nut fudge, pecan praline fudge royale, chocolate amaretto truffles, chocolate butter rum truffles—You won't believe the list! Guests are welcome to visit the unusual chapel. (Brigittine Monks Gourmet Confections, 23300 Walker Lane, Amity; 503-835-8080.)

Leaving the monastery, return to the Bellevue Highway, which dead ends at Highway 18. At this T-junction, you are looking across the road to the Lawrence Gallery and the **Oregon Wine Tasting Room**. This is Oregon's oldest tasting room, and it's stocked with some 100 or so wines from vineyards all across the state. (19706 SW Highway 18; open from 11:30 am to 5:30 pm daily; 503-843-3787.) After a browse through it, take Hwy 18 back to 99W North/McMinnville. As you're heading out of McMinnville, turn left onto 47 North/Carlton. Pass through Carlton and follow the signs for 47/Yamhill/Forest Grove as it zigzags you through town.

Once in **Gaston**, turn left on Olson Road to **Elk Cove Vineyards**, whose beautiful setting is alone worth the trip. Here, winemaker Adam Campbell produces single-vineyard Pinot Noir, Pinot Gris, Dijon-clone Chardonnay, Riesling, Cabernet Sauvignon, and highly popular dessert wines. (27751 NW Olson Road; open from 11 am to 5 pm daily; 503-985-7760.) Leaving Elk Cove, resume your former course on 47 North. The road will make a left turn. Just follow signs to Hwy 8; further on 8, take east City Center/Portland all the way back to the city.

SCENIC COLUMBIA RIVER HIGHWAY AND MOUNT HOOD LOOP

The Columbia River Gorge National Scenic Area stretches about 80 miles from Troutdale (just 20 minutes east of Portland) to the Deschutes River east of The Dalles, and one of the best ways to see it is from the **Historic Columbia River Highway** (old US 30). This highway was constructed between 1913 and 1922 in a European style to conform to the contours of the land and take full advantage of the spectacular scenery. It is accessible today in two short stretches (one of 22 miles from Troutdale to Ainsworth State Park, the other a 16-mile stretch from Mosier to The Dalles, with a 35-mile section along the main interstate in between). We'll concentrate on the first 22-mile stretch before taking you on a loop around Mount Hood and back to Portland. Plan to linger in this magnificent part of the state as we guide you past waterfalls, through lush state parks, to dramatic vistas from cliffs dropping 700 to 2,000 feet into the river. Consider packing a picnic lunch so you can stop where you like, to soak in the surroundings.

From Portland, take I-84 east to our first stop off Exit 17: **Troutdale**. Exit and drive along the frontage road to Graham Road (follow signs for Troutdale and Columbia River Highway), where you'll turn right. Take your first left on Columbia River Highway and drive directly into town, where a short stretch of galleries, shops, and museums beckons you to stop and browse. Troutdale, which traces its origins to the arrival of the railroad in 1882, started as a thriving agricultural community and has since grown to become home to some 9,000 residents. A visitor center, on the main road here, is a good place to inquire about trails in nearby Sandy River Canyon and Beaver Creek Canyon, or to find out more about activities in the area generally. An imposing bronze likeness of Nez Perce Chief Joseph graces a small plaza. One favorite stop in Troutdale is **McMenamins Edgefield**, a 38-acre estate originally built in 1911 as the Multnomah County Poor Farm and now on the National Register of Historic Places. Visitors come to relive history through tours of the renovated buildings and grounds. It's quite a complex, if a bit commercialized. You'll find a brewery and beer garden, a winery and tasting room, a golf course, a movie theater crafted from a 1930's boiler room, restaurants, a gift shop, herb and vegetable gardens, and hostel-like accommodations. To get to it, turn right off of Graham Road (which you took from Exit 17), then right onto Columbia River Highway, rather than left into downtown Troutdale. The road veers left to become NE Halsey and Edgefield is on your left.

Once you've had as much or as little of Edgefield as suits your fancy, head back into and through the town of Troutdale, cross the Sandy River Bridge, and veer right to begin the Columbia River Highway. Climb uphill to the town of **Springdale**. Stop at **Mom's Garden Bakery** (the *big* blue house on the right) for Patty Meyers' amazing homemade fruit Danish, brioche, and other goodies. Continue on to **Corbett** and your first astounding view of the gorge at the **Portland Women's Forum State Park at Chanticleer Point**. Everything is well marked. This is the former site of the Chanticleer Inn, where the highway's visionaries met in 1913 to plan its construction. Samuel C. Lancaster, design engineer of the highway, picked the next spot, **Crown Point,** expressly for its potential as a prime observation point. He hired Edgar Lazarus to design **Vista House** (1918), a gray sandstone octagon building, offering stellar views from the observatory deck at the top of a narrow staircase. (Open daily from 8:30 am to 6 pm, April to mid October.) While the Vista House itself could stand some upgrade attention, you won't mind once you're gazing at the Columbia some 700 feet below.

Back in the car, you'll now head into a mossy wonderland of rain forest and have, within a very few miles, your choice of footpaths to waterfalls. The first is **Latourell**, offering the shortest distance from the road to the falls; next is **Shepperd's Dell**, which can only be viewed once you pull over and step onto a bridge. We recommend driving to **Bridal Veil** and venturing the short ⅔-mile trail to the falls if you've got sturdy footwear and don't mind the sometimes steep and often rugged terrain. Back in the 1880s, this beautiful spot was home to the Bridal Veil Lumber Company, who produced boxes for everything from apples to WWII ammunition to cheese and operated until 1980. Keep your eye out for an easier ¼-mile path to the cliff for stunning views of the gorge. Only the noisy I-84 detracts from this otherwise beautiful spot.

Next you come to two-tiered, 620-foot **Multnomah Falls** and the **Multnomah Falls Lodge** (1925). Likely to be crowded in summer months, it's still

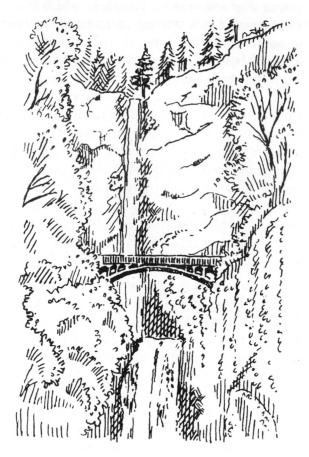

Multnomah Falls

worth at least pulling over to see it from your car. The adventurous can take a ½-mile trail up from the lodge to a bridge that crosses the lower cascade, then continue to the top via switchbacks. The lodge itself is beautiful, now housing an information center, a gift shop, and a restaurant. (Hours vary; 503-695-2376.)

From Multnomah Falls, you'll have to join I-84 again. Take Exit 40 to the **Bonneville Dam**, built by the federal government for $70 million between 1933 and 1936 at the urging of Franklin D. Roosevelt. It's an impressive piece of engineering, to be sure. The five-story **Bradford Island Visitor Center** (open daily from 9 am to 5 pm) features exhibits discussing the purpose and building of the dam; as well as films about the Columbia River, fish migration, and current U.S. Army Corps of Engineers' projects. If you've never seen a fish ladder, this is a good place to experience it: through an underwater window you can watch salmon and other fish bypass the dam as they follow nature's migratory course unimpeded.

Back on I-84, take Exit 44, Cascade Locks/Stevenson/Hwy 30. Docked at the Port of **Cascade Locks** is the historic **Sternwheeler Columbia Gorge Steamer**. Although, riverboat trips are offered only seasonally, this is an entertaining way to explore the river. (800-643-1354, www.cascadelocks.net) From the waterfront, follow the signs to the **Bridge of the Gods** and cross over to the state of Washington. Take 14 east for a few hundred yards, then turn left on Rock Creek Drive. Turn left again onto the **Skamania Lodge** property and consider having lunch (informal, cafeteria-style) in the huge dining room with windows for walls and great views (509-427-7700). If you're ready to return to Portland, take Hwy 14 all the way back for a different and dramatic view of the gorge's high basalt cliffs, meandering your way through tall forests of trees and past several trailheads and scenic pullouts, including the beautiful **Cape Horn** lookout. This side of the river is considerably less crowded.

If you're up for more, however, cross the Bridge of the Gods again to return to the Oregon side and take I-84 east to Exit 64. Head south on 35, and turn left on Old Columbia River Drive. Follow signs to the **Columbia River Highway State Trail (Senator Mark O. Hatfield West Trailhead)**. This section of the Columbia River Highway stretches between Hood River and Mosier farther east. Once accessible to vehicles, it has since been transformed into a unique, public footpath running just over

4½ miles. You can walk or bicycle or roller skate as much, or as little, of it as you like. It's relatively easy, well-paved, and graced by two "in-line" or "twin" tunnels, the **Mosier Twin Tunnels**, originally constructed in 1919 and 1920 to make it possible for the highway to pass through a steep basalt bluff. The West Tunnel is only 81 feet in length; the East Tunnel is 288 feet. Windows cut into the rock allow for terrific gorge views. This is a one-of-a-kind trail! Keep in mind that the Mosier Tunnels are closer to the Mosier end of the trail. If you prefer a short walk (about 2 miles round) to the tunnels and back, you can drive to that end of the trailhead instead (take Exit 69/Mosier, turn right at the end of the off ramp, then take your first left on Rock Creek Road and follow signs to the trailhead). It's a great walk through lava beds and forest, all overlooking the gorge. Notice the signatures carved into the north wall of the East Tunnel, where in 1921 a handful of people found themselves snowbound for several cold November days.

Make a visit to **Hood River**, a casual and friendly community of windsurfers and breweries, and one of Oregon's major apple- and pear-growing regions. Consider a **Mount Hood Railroad** excursion, departing from the Hood River Depot and offering a four-hour, scenic round trip through the gently beautiful Hood River Valley, with a stop in quaint Parkdale. The railroad, dating back to 1906, was once used to serve local farmers, transporting fruit from area orchards to the city. Choose from morning, afternoon, and evening rides; some including brunch or dinner as an option. (110 Railroad Avenue; hours vary; 541-386-3556.) Carousel enthusiasts may enjoy the unique and comprehensive collection at **The International Museum of Carousel Art**. (304 Oak Street; open Wednesday to Sunday from noon to 4 pm; 541-387-4622.) There is also a good selection of restaurants in Hood River.

If you are staying in the Hood River/Mount Hood area, there's a wonderful scenic mini-loop we highly recommend. Affectionately called the "**Fruit Loop**" by locals, it follows Hwy 35 South from Exit 64/Hood River, heads west at Mount Hood through Parkdale, and picks up the Dee Hwy, or Hwy 281, back northward to I-84, just west of Hood River. When you are ready to resume our tour, head south on Hwy 35 from Hood River to begin the **Mount Hood Loop Highway**, which circles the eastern shoulder of Mount Hood and passes through lovely fruit orchards, flower farms, and, eventually, the mountainous wilderness of the Cascades at Barlow Pass (4,157 feet), part of the original Oregon Trail. Allow time to pull off the road at spots that speak to you. In season, gather fruit at one of many "U-Pick" fruit farms along the route.

Mount Hood is Oregon's highest peak at 11,235 feet. Thirty or so miles past the town of Mount Hood, turn right off Hwy 35 (which you'll notice has become Hwy 26) to the famed **Timberline Lodge** (1936–37), a National Historic Landmark and masterpiece of mountain lodge architecture. Constructed of enormous local timbers and native stone, the lodge is a rugged example of the handmade American Arts and Crafts movement of the '30s. It caters to skiers and provides a grandly rustic Cascade Dining Room. (Open year round; 503-622-7979.) One of the state's premier hiking trails is the 40-mile **Timberline Trail**, which loops around Mount Hood and provides unparalleled views of the Cascade Mountains, the Willamette Valley, and meadows of wildflowers. August and September are the best months for walking. For information on how to get the most out of the trail in short excursions, call the Hood River Ranger District at 541-352-6002 or inquire in the lodge.

Retrace your steps back to Hwy 26, and continue westward to Portland to complete this round trip.

MOUNT ST. HELENS NATIONAL VOLCANIC MONUMENT DAY TRIP

Only 40,000 years old, **Mount St. Helens** is the baby of the southern Cascade volcano family in an area where all the peaks are seismically active. On May 18, 1980, following two months of small earthquakes and relatively mild eruptions, one particular trembler loosened much of the north flank of this mountain. An avalanche ensued, after which a huge blast cloud roared out of the crater, outracing the avalanche as it reached speeds of up to 600 mph. A hot, stone-filled wind knocked down immense forests in its path, creating a litter of fallen trees in a "blowdown zone" still visible today. This initial destruction took only five minutes; but for nine hours afterward, a column of ash spewed 15 miles high from the crater, obscuring eastern Washington. Melted glaciers created mudflows and severe flooding, 57 people were suddenly dead or missing, and Mount St. Helens had dropped in elevation by 1,300 feet. This is something you should see.

From Portland, take I-5 north 50 miles to Exit 49/Hwy 504. Known as the Spirit Lake Memorial Highway, 504 was constructed between 1992 and 1995. It's about 48 miles long and guides you, more or less, alongside the path of destruction, all the way to the volcano itself. The blowdown zone is perhaps one of the most awe-inspiring sights, where trees still lie scattered like giant toothpicks. Your first stop, however, is about 5 miles east of the freeway exit. *Not* the giant blue building just off the freeway called the Cinedome (misguidedly called the Visitor Center), but rather a park building further down the road called the **Mount St. Helens Visitor Center**. It provides an excellent introduction to the area, with many marvelous exhibits and a slide presentation. We recommend you pay for the pass that gives you unrestricted access to all the centers along the route to the volcano. From the Visitor Center, continue along 504 and stop at any, or all, of the additional visitor centers you might be interested in. The Charles W. Bingham Forest Learning Center concentrates on the life cycle of area forests and features an impressive elk-viewing area with great views, while the Coldwater Ridge Visitor Center focuses on the recovery of the surroundings and the new lakes that were formed by the eruption. Rangers give brief lectures on related topics. The "must see" is the **Johnston Ridge Observatory**, only 5 miles from the volcano. Named for a geologist who lost his life in the final blast, the observatory offers an amazing view of Mount St. Helens and a 15-minute film called *A Message from the Mountain*, which will stop you in your tracks.

For a closer look at the volcano, you can take a helicopter tour to the crater or walk along several trails, one of the more dramatic ones beginning at the Johnston Ridge Observatory.

When you are ready to return to Portland, simply retrace your steps as there is no loop available.

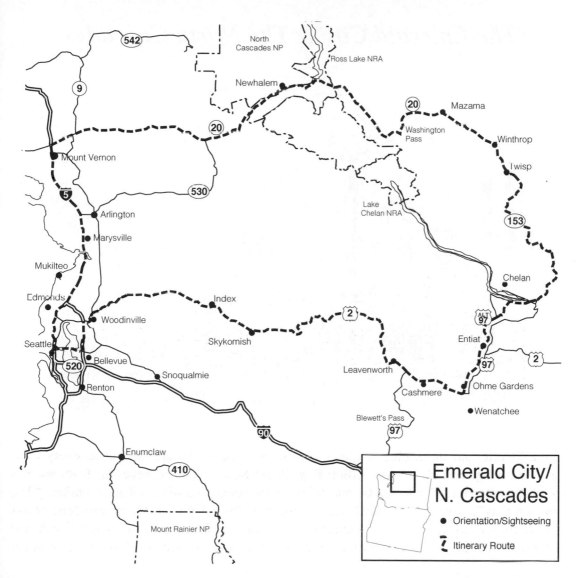

542

9

North
Cascades NP

Ross Lake NRA

Newhalem

20

Mazama

20

Washington
Pass

Winthrop

Mount Vernon

Twisp

5

530

153

Arlington

Lake
Chelan NRA

Marysville

Mukilteo

Chelan

Edmonds

Index

2

ALT
97

Woodinville

Entiat

Seattle

Skykomish

97

2

Bellevue

Leavenworth

Ohme Gardens

520

Snoqualmie

Cashmere

Renton

Wenatchee

Blewett's Pass

97

90

Enumclaw

410

Mount Rainier NP

Emerald City/
N. Cascades

● Orientation/Sightseeing

⌇ Itinerary Route

The Emerald City & The North Cascades

Seattle

Think Seattle and think blue. Endless wide-open spaces of water appear at every turn: Lake Washington, Lake Union, Elliott Bay, Puget Sound. You're never far from water's soothing influence. Think Seattle and think green (hence its affectionate moniker, "The Emerald City"), where trees, parks, and woodlands abound even as the urban scene grows to ever-increasing levels of 21st-century sophistication. Characteristic of the Northwest generally, Seattle's culture is friendly and casual, its pace relatively slow, its style never one to take itself too seriously. Like Portland, it is a city passionate about nature, devoted to ensuring that its gorgeous surroundings remain an integral part of city life rather than something to overcome. Hence you will always have Mount Rainer, Mount Baker, the Olympics, and the majestic Cascades within view. Initially little more than a logging town, Seattle has evolved over a period of 150 years to become one of America's key urban destinations. It's the perfect spot from which to explore much of western and central Washington's immense beauty: its rich cultural life, its mountain ranges, its wineries, its ancient lava flows, its islands, and its close neighbor, British Columbia.

Recommended Pacing: If you have the time, take at least three days to explore Seattle. Also, all of the excursions in this section are trips designed to begin and end in Seattle for the most convenient approach. The Wine Country tour can easily be accomplished as a day trip from Seattle; but there are outstanding inns and restaurants in Bellevue and Woodinville, so we urge you to consider a luxurious overnight at one of them. The North Cascades excursion can take as little as two days, if you just make a round trip to Leavenworth; while you should allow at least four nights and five days to complete the entire loop itinerary at a leisurely pace.

SEATTLE

Like most cities, **Seattle** is ideally approached on foot, one neighborhood at a time, rather than fighting your way on unfamiliar one-way mazes in traffic. Consider taking cabs between the neighborhoods you want to explore (distances are not great) or using public transportation—the Seattle Metropolitan Transit System operates buses and trolleys throughout the city and its suburbs. Ask your innkeeper, always your most valuable resource, for tips on getting around easily, depending on what you want to do.

Visitors bureaus are always a good first stop for getting oriented. Stop in at the **Seattle-King County Convention & Visitors Bureau** for maps, sightseeing ideas, and schedules of current in-town events. The bureau is located at the Washington State Convention & Trade Center, 800 Convention Place on the Galleria Level. (Open weekdays from 8:30 am to 5 pm, weekend hours vary seasonally; 206-461-5840; *www.seeseattle.org*.)

The **Seattle Art Museum** is a city landmark now, with its signature *Hammering Man*, 48 feet tall, poised to greet you at the entrance. It houses a permanent collection of some 23,000 pieces representing a wide range of art, from ancient Egyptian reliefs to contemporary American installations using photography and video. Of particular note are its collections of Asian, African, and Northwest Coast Native American art, as well as its European paintings. The complete collection actually resides in two separate locations. The majority of it is located in downtown Seattle (100 University Street) in the contemporary building we've been talking about; but if you are especially appreciative of Asian art, you shouldn't miss the impressive collection on Capitol Hill in Volunteer Park (1400 E. Prospect Street). Housed in a building designed in 1933 by Seattle architect, Carl Gould, and known as the **Seattle Asian Art Museum**, this collection is credited as one of the top ten of its kind in the entire U.S., with an eclectic assortment of art from Japan, China, Korea, India, the Himalayas, and Southeast Asia. (Seattle Art Museum hours: Tuesday to Sunday from 10 am to 5 pm, except Thursday from 10 am to 9 pm; 206-654-3255. Asian Art Museum hours: Wednesday to Sunday from 10 am to 5 pm, except Thursday from 10 am to 9 pm; 206-654-3206. Web address for both museums: *www.seattleartmuseum.org*.)

Across the street from the Seattle Art Museum is the **Harbor Steps**, a popular spot for open-air concerts in summer months and a great place for people watching. Take the steps down to the waterfront and enjoy a stroll along Elliott Bay.

Museum enthusiasts will also enjoy the **Frye Art Museum** at 704 Terry Avenue (corner of Cherry Street). Children of German emigrants who rose to prominence in the Seattle of the late 19th century, Charles and Emma Frye owned and operated a large-scale meat processing plant with retail outlets that stretched from California to Alaska. During this prosperous time, the Fryes were able to travel extensively and indulge their passion for collecting artwork. They purchased their first European painting at the Chicago World's Fair in 1893, and from then on became serious collectors of realist art. Their collection of 19th- and 20th-century paintings grew to more than 230 works in their lifetime. Each piece is on view at the museum today, including the most complete collection of Munich

School paintings in this country. (Open Tuesday to Saturday from 10 am to 5 pm, except Thursday from 10 am to 9 pm, plus Sunday from noon to 4 pm; 206-622-9250; *www.fryeart.org*.)

Pike Place Market

You've certainly heard about **Pike Place Market** (bounded by 1st Avenue, Western Avenue, Pike Street, and Virginia Street). Situated on 9 acres of now-protected land, it all began in 1907 when the city decided to single out a place where local farmers could sell their produce direct to consumers. The idea caught on in a big way, and today this public market is something more of a cross between a farmers' market and a carnival. Take all the time you want to browse among the stalls of vegetables, meats, cheeses, flowers, and baubles. Look sharp around the fish stands, where one vendor is likely to throw a whole fish to the other right over your head as they wrap it to order. (Open from 10 am to 6 pm, Monday to Saturday, and from 11 am to 5 pm Sunday; 206-682-7453.) A popular staircase here is called the **Pike Street Hill Climb**, whose stairs will take you to the waterfront activity along Elliott Bay. Watch for signs in the marketplace directing you there.

The family-run **Elliott Bay Book Company** at 101 S. Main Street is a delightful bookstore, in operation since 1973 and a refreshing alternative to the large chains, with its cedar shelves, exposed brick, and café. (Open Monday to Thursday from 10 am to 10 pm, Friday and Saturday from 10 am to 11 pm, Sunday from 11 am to 7 pm, and holidays from noon to 5 pm; 800-962-5311; *www.elliottbaybook.com*.)

Pioneer Square traces its start to the mid-19th-century logging days of early Seattle. It's a small area of only a few blocks, including the original "Skid Road" (Yesler Way), later popularly known as "**Skid Row**," where logs were literally slid downhill to the local sawmill for cutting and shipping. **Pioneer Place** (1st Avenue and Yesler Way) is best known for its Seattle landmarks: a Tlingit totem pole reproduction, a wrought-iron pergola constructed in 1909 to shelter passengers waiting for streetcars, and the Pioneer Building, a six-story Romanesque Revival structure constructed in 1892. For a fascinating and unusual introduction to the salty history of young Seattle in this area, take **Bill Speidel's Underground Tour**. It's an adventurous, 90-minute walking tour beneath today's street level, for that's where the original downtown Seattle was located before the Great Fire of 1889. Learn all about it as you marvel at the building fronts of hundred-year-old brothels, shops, dance halls, and emporiums. It's fun, but not for the claustrophobic. (608 First Avenue between Yesler & Cherry; hours vary monthly; 206-682-4646; *www.undergroundtour.com*.)

Following an underground tour, you might be in the mood for a very different view of the area. Make your way to **Seattle Center**, just north of downtown and bounded to the southeast by Broad Street, the 74-acre site of the 1962 World's Fair. (A fun way to get there is by monorail from Westlake Center Mall at 5th Avenue and Pine Street.) Take the glass elevator to the top of the 602-foot **Space Needle**, where indoor and outdoor observation decks provide a magnificent 360-degree view of the area, weather permitting as usual, and a revolving restaurant serves first-class, Pacific Northwest cuisine. (Open from 8 am to midnight in summer; otherwise from 9 am to 11 pm weekdays, to midnight weekends; 206-905-2100, *www.spaceneedle.com*.) Other attractions at the center include an **amusement park**, the very hands-on **Pacific Science Center** (open from 10 am to 5 pm weekdays, to 6 pm weekends; 206-443-2001; *www.pacsci.org*) and **Children's Museum** (open from 10 am to 5 pm weekdays, to 6 pm weekends; 206-441-1768; *www.thechildrensmuseum.org*), and several theaters.

If you have children in your party, they will probably enjoy a visit to the **Woodland Park Zoo**, also at the north end of the city, with its hundreds of rare and endangered animals, African Village, and adorable young Asian elephant born in November 2000. Other attractions include two Sumatran tigers born in December of 2002. (5500 Phinney Avenue North; open daily at 9:30 am—call for seasonal closing times; 206-684-4800; *www.zoo.org*.)

Next to the zoo is a beautiful **rose garden**, with 280 varieties and over 5,000 individual plants. This is one of 24 test gardens in the United States.

Just north of downtown, Puget Sound is joined to Lake Washington by an 8-mile ship canal and a system of locks that bisect the city from west to east. Named for a Brigadier General in the U.S. Army Corps of Engineers, the **Hiram M. Chittenden Locks** and **Canal** were completed in 1917, allowing ships access inland to the then-coveted coal and timber resources on the eastern shores of Lake Washington. A **Visitors Center** at 3015 NW 54th Street features displays on the history of these structures and on the details of its current operation. (Hours vary seasonally: call 206-783-7059.) If you've never seen a lock in action, this is a good place to discover it for the first time. Some 100,000 boats of all different types pass through the lock system each year.

If you venture to the Asian Art Museum, take a walk over to the nearby **Capitol Hill Water Tower**, also in Volunteer Park. You can't miss it; it's a circular brick structure, towering above you to a height of about 75 feet. From the top of the tower you'll have an amazing panoramic view of the area. There's also an interesting exhibit in the tower about the work of the Olmsted brothers, designers of Seattle's more elegant parks. The formal gardens of the 43-acre **Volunteer Park** (E. Prospect Street between 11th and 15th Avenues East) are representative of the work of the Olmsteds, but a truer example of their inspired philosophy (preserving views of the magnificent surroundings whenever possible) is best seen from East Garfield Street. Exit Volunteer Park on its eastern side and make your way north to **East Garfield**. From here, you will happen upon one of the most picturesque views of Lake Washington, the Evergreen Point Floating Bridge and the Cascade Mountains, from a unique roost designed by the brothers.

Washington Park Arboretum offers a great number of wonderful walking trails through woodlands and specialty areas celebrating different plants in concentration: honeysuckle, azaleas, rhododendrons, dogwood, decorative cherry trees, and a Japanese garden. (2300 Arboretum Drive East; open from 8 am to dusk; 206-543-8800.)

The **University of Washington** campus makes for a charming walking tour as well. Pick up a **Campus Walk** booklet at the **Visitor Information Center** at 4014 University Way NE at NE Campus Parkway (open from 8 am to 5 pm weekdays; 206-543-9198). You can also download the walking tour from *www.washington.edu*. Click on "Visitors," then "Tours On Campus," then "A Campus Walk." This self-guided tour will take you along wide pedestrian thoroughfares, past lovely landscaped gardens, and by buildings of significance to the university, identifying everything for you. The on-campus **Henry Art Gallery** at 15th Avenue NE and NE 41st Street is considered one of the country's most progressive, small museums dedicated to modern and contemporary art. The Henry's permanent collection of over 20,000 objects includes late 19th- and 20th-century paintings, an extensive Monsen Collection of Photography, and a textile and costume collection, along with a burgeoning compilation of cutting-edge works in new media. (Open Tuesday to Sunday from 11 am to 5 pm, except Thursday from 11 am to 8 pm; 206-543-2280.)

Also of note on campus is the excellent **Burke Museum of Natural History and Culture** at NE 45th Street and 17th Avenue NE. The Burke contains collections totaling over 3 million specimens. These collections are divided into three main divisions: Geology, Anthropology, and Zoology. We were moved by an exhibition called *The Endurance: Shackleton's Legendary Antarctic Expedition*, the story of Shackleton's infamous 1914 journey to Antarctica as told through diary excerpts, film footage, and haunting photographs by the expedition's photographer. (Open daily from 10 am to 5 pm except Thursday till 8 pm; 206-543-5590; *www.washington.edu/burkemuseum*.)

The largest air and space museum in the western U.S. is found here in Seattle. Housed in soaring spaces of steel and glass, the **Museum of Flight** is located at 9404 Marginal Way South (a half-mile northwest of the city on I-5 at Exit 158). It records the story of man's air and space achievements in an awe-inspiring setting, combining marvelous, interactive exhibits with actual artifacts. The Great Gallery Complex alone contains more than 50 aircraft, 20 or more suspended above your head! (Open daily from 10 am to 5 pm, except the first Thursday of each month till 9 pm; 206-764-5720; *www.museumofflight.org*.)

SEATTLE WINE COUNTRY TOUR

Washington is now the second-largest producer of premium wines in the United States, with more than 150 wineries and over 25,000 acres of vineyards. Second only to California in wine production, Washington prides itself on producing some of the finest red, white, and fruit wines.

As it happens, the 46°N parallel runs through the wine-growing regions of Bordeaux, Burgundy, and eastern Washington; drawing many comparisons between Washington wines and French wines. The diverse climate of eastern Washington, ranging from long, warm summer days to cool nights, ensures that Washington wineries produce a wide variety of wines, including Cabernet Sauvignon, Merlot, Sauvignon Blanc, Semillon, Pinot Gris, Chardonnay, Riesling, Gewürztraminer, Lemberger, Chenin Blanc, and Syrah.

Fortunately, it's not necessary to drive 200 miles to the eastern portions of the state, where most vineyards are located, for this tour will take you to some of the finest tasting rooms just minutes from Seattle.

From Seattle, take Hwy 520 east across Lake Washington, then head north on I-405 toward Bothell for about 12 miles. Exit at 522 east/**Woodinville**. Turn right on 175th Street, then left at the stop sign onto Hwy 202 (also known as the Woodinville-Redmond Road and later, NE 145th). Our first stop is the humble home of **Silver Lake Winery**.

Silver Lake holds the distinction as Washington's only "consumer-owned" winery: hundreds of Northwest enthusiasts have pooled their resources to build this award winner. You could join them! Try their handcrafted varietals, in production since 1989, or their Spire Mountain hard fruit ciders. (15029 Woodinville-Redmond Road/Hwy 202; open daily from noon to 5 pm; 425-486-1900; *www.silverlakewinery.com*.)

Our next stop around the bend (where the Woodinville-Redmond Road veers left to become NE 145th) is **Columbia Winery**. Watch for it on your left. Founded in 1962 by ten friends, six of whom were professors at the University of Washington, Columbia Winery is considered Washington's first premium winery. First known as Associated Vintners, the group was keen to prove that Washington could produce high-quality wines and began in the Seattle garage of one of the professors. Today, winemaker David Lake, often referred to as the "Dean of Washington Wine" (*Wine Spectator*), continues the founders' tradition of innovation by introducing new varietals to the state, including Syrah, Cabernet Franc, Pinot Gris, and Sangiovese. Wines from Columbia Winery are known for the rich, fruit flavors indicative of Washington. (14030 NE 145th; open from 10 am to 7 pm daily; 425-488-2776; *www.columbiawinery.com*.)

Virtually across the street from Columbia is our next stop, **Chateau Ste. Michelle**, which has been producing European varietal wines since 1967. It is best known for its award-winning Chardonnay, Merlot, and Cabernet Sauvignon. Its white wines are fermented and aged right in Woodinville, while its reds are made in eastern Washington just west of Paterson on the Columbia River. The facilities and grounds here (87 acres) are beautiful, with peacocks strutting around on the lawns. In 1912, Seattle lumber baron Frederick Stimson made his home here, with gardens designed by the Olmsteds, the same family responsible for Seattle's Volunteer Park and New York City's Central Park. Now on the National Register of Historic Places, Stimson's home is used for special events. A variety of tour, tasting, and event options are yours, including wine appreciation seminars and a summer concert series (Summer Festival on the Green) to benefit the arts. (14111 NE 145th; open from 10 am to 4:30 pm daily; 425-488-1133; *www.chateau-stemichelle.com*.)

Continue down NE 145th to **Redhook Brewery** for the brew masters in your group. Beer enthusiasts Paul Shipman and Gordon Bowker founded Redhook in Seattle in 1981, at a time when the import beer market was growing by leaps and bounds in the Northwest. They sold their first pint of ale in August of 1982; then in July 1994, Redhook completed its second brewery here in Woodinville. This handsome facility features expansive grounds including the Forecasters Public House, where you can indulge in all of the Redhook Ales, as well as pub-style meals. Brewery tours cost $1 per person and include three to four samples of beer, a souvenir tasting glass, a walk through the brewery, and a good dose of Redhook history. (14300 NE 145th Street; Redhook Brewery open daily from 2 to 4 pm on weekdays, and from noon to 5 pm on weekends; The Forecasters Pub is open daily from 11 am to 9 pm on Sundays, from 11 am to 11 pm on Mondays through Thursdays, and from 11 am to midnight on Fridays and Saturdays; 425-483-3232; *www.redhook.com*.)

The popular **Burke Gilman Trail**, a 34-mile walking/bicycling/horse trail, passes right in front of the Willows Lodge and these two restaurants. It follows the Sammamish River to the edge of Lake Washington, then continues on around the lake to the University of Washington and out to Puget Sound. Continue along NE 145th, cross the Sammamish River, and turn right onto the Woodinville-Redmond Road heading south. This road will take you through some lovely rural countryside into the town of Redmond, from which you'll pick up 520 back to Seattle via Bellevue.

NORTH CASCADES LOOP

This spectacular scenic loop can be approached in several different ways. If time is of the essence, we recommend at least the gorgeous, 105-mile drive along Hwy 2 from Seattle, out over the Cascade Mountains, and into the town of Leavenworth for a one- or two-night stay, returning to the city via the same route. In late September/early October, the maples and yellow larches in Tumwater Canyon, just northwest of Leavenworth along this route, will take your breath away. If you can afford the luxury of more time, follow this complete itinerary, which will take you past Leavenworth, guide you north through working fruit orchards, and loop you westward again—weather permitting—through the dramatic North Cascades National Park. Keep in mind that the stretch of Hwy 20 just west of Mazama (between Washington Pass and Rainy Pass) is closed for long periods during winter, spring, and (sometimes) early summer, so be sure to check road conditions before attempting to cross.

North Cascades Highway

The Emerald City & The North Cascades

From Seattle, take Hwy 520 east to I-405 North to Hwy 522 east to Hwy 2 east. The road to **Leavenworth** is absolutely beautiful. Surrounded by some of the most stunning scenery anywhere in the U.S., this town was once home to the Yakima, Chinook, and Wenatchee Indian tribes. By 1890, the original town was built and settled by pioneers in search of gold, fur, and fertile farmland. At the turn of the 19th century, the Great Northern Railway brought additional prosperity; but it was not to last—the unexpected re-routing of the railroad and the subsequent closure of the area's sawmill reduced Leavenworth to something of a ghost town. For more than 30 years, it lived on the brink of extinction; then, in the early 1960s, community leaders got the idea to change Leavenworth's appearance. Inspired by the beautiful backdrop of the surrounding Alpine mountains, the town agreed to remodel their hamlet in the form of a Bavarian village. The entire community rallied to create the illusion of Bavaria in the middle of Washington State!

Besides the complete renovation of the downtown area, the town has created a series of festivals that brings tourists from miles around, including the Autumn Leaf Festival, Maifest, and the extremely popular Christmas Lighting Ceremony. While the town itself may well strike you as a bit over the top, give in to it for a day or two—you won't find a friendlier or more beautiful spot anywhere. Stay at any one of the excellent inns in town and enjoy the spectacular setting. Innkeepers here can recommend stellar, short-distance driving routes (e.g., taking 97 South to **Old Blewetts Pass** for unparalleled views), great river-rafting trips, and breathtaking hiking trails you won't want to miss.

From Leavenworth, travel east on Hwy 2 in the direction of Wenatchee. The small town of **Cashmere**, is known for its famous **Liberty Orchards-Aplets and Cotlets** factory and store (509-782-4088, www.libertyorchards.com), and the outdoor **Pioneer Village Museum** (509-782-3230) replicating life in the 1800s. It is also home to a wonderful bakery that is most definitely worth a stop for its wonderful baked products, sandwiches and coffees. **Anjou Bakery** (509-782-4360) is located beyond the entrance to town, on the south side of the highway.

A few miles beyond, Cashmere Hwy 2 merges with Hwy 97 which, if you follow north, will take you on to Chelan. If you are a garden buff, you might want to detour just at the merger of the two highways to visit **Ohme Gardens**. Located high on a rocky bluff, overlooking the confluence of the Columbia and Weneatchee Rivers, this nine-acre garden is a result of one family and 60 years of dedicated landscaping.

There are actually two "versions" of the highway that straddle both sides of the river. Alt 97, as opposed to the Hwy2/97, is the more scenic drive and more easily accesses the road to Lake Chelan. This is a region dominated by pear and apple orchards, absolutely gorgeous when colored with spring blossoms or fall foliage; but to be honest, a little barren in winter. Many of the Washington apples you buy in stores come from this very area. Alt 97 will take you directly to **Lake Chelan**, a 50-mile-long lake in a beautiful valley created by glaciers. Reaching a depth of 1,500 feet, it is one of the deepest lakes in the U.S. Or you can also opt for Hwy 971, referred to as the Navarre Coulee cutoff which is a few miles longer, but crests the hill and affords some wonderful views of the lake.

From Lake Chelan, continue north on Hwy 97 to Hwy 153, and then to Hwy 20, traveling in the direction of Winthrop. Spring through fall, Hwy 20 would deliver you back to the coast, but in winter it dead-ends at Washington Pass. With the towering peaks of the Cascades looming in the distance, Hwy 20 travels a picturesque route through a beautiful valley, following the wide sweep of river that cuts it. It is a region populated by large ranches, grazed by cattle and reportedly the source of inspiration for poet and author Owen Wister. He lived in **Winthrop** back in the early 1900s, and many Winthrop sights and characters appear in his novel *The Virginian*. Today, this once-busy mining town is little more than a faux Old West façade, with wooden sidewalks and early 20th-century storefronts. You might enjoy the **Shafer Museum**, though, which re-creates a turn of the century pioneer mining town. Nine buildings (some reproductions, others original and relocated here) offer a glimpse of life in the Cascades more than a hundred years ago. (Castle and Corral Avenues; open May to September, Thursday to Monday, from 10 am to 5 pm.)

The **North Cascades Highway** (Hwy 20) offers a unique opportunity to explore some of the more remote areas of the Cascade Mountains. Some 300 glaciers residing here account for more than half the glaciers in the contiguous United States. Along the way, a number of trailhead markers will beckon you to stop and explore, which is fun to do even if you hike for only short distances. Two mountain passes greet you now. The first is **Washington Pass** at 5,477 feet. Pull over at the **lookout** and take the half-mile (round trip) path around a cliff face to see just how far you've come! The second is 4,860-foot **Rainy Pass**. An easy 2-mile (round trip) paved trail at Rainy Pass is perfect if you're conscious of time or don't want to do any serious walking. Watch for signs for the **Rainy Lake Trail** and pull over. The trail will guide you through towering forest to the small, and unbelievably, blue **Rainy Lake**. Notice how the terrain is changing. These mountain passes mark the rain shadow divide that accounts for one climate in western Washington and another east of the mountains.

About 1 mile west of Newhalem, the **North Cascades Visitors Center's** audio-visual presentations offer a variety of points of view on the area. Take the short wood-planked path behind the center to a viewpoint overlooking the beautiful Picket Range. Continue west on Hwy 20 to return to I-5 and you'll be back to Seattle in about an hour.

Alternate Side Trip: If you can extend your journey, rather than return to Seattle, you might want to consider heading south across the Oregon border and follow our recommendations along the Columbia River. It takes about five hours to cover the distance to the Columbia Gorge.

From Leavenworth, it is an easy and beautiful drive taking Hwy 97 up the forested valley, across the **Blewett Pass**, down Hwy 90 and east to the university town of **Ellensburg**. The numerous, red brick buildings reflect the history of the town. Back in 1898, on the eve of a public vote to determine whether Ellensburg or Olympia would be the capital of Washington, the town of Ellensburg burnt to the ground; and by default, Olympia became the seat of government. Conservatively, when Ellensburg was rebuilt, brick replaced wood.

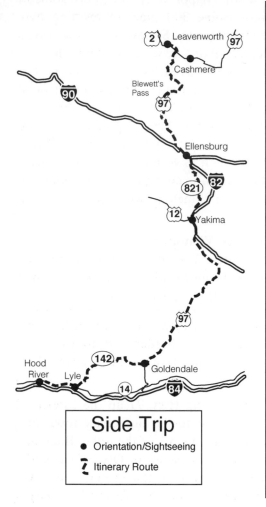

Side Trip

- Orientation/Sightseeing
- Itinerary Route

Just outside of Ellensburg jog onto Hwy 82, and then take Route 821 that follows the path of the Yakima River, a beautiful drive through this undeveloped River Canyon. This is reputed to be one of the best areas for spotting bald eagles, osprey and hawk. The 821 rejoins the 82 just north of Yakima, referred to as the "Palm Springs of Washington."

Continue on Hwy 82, twenty miles southeast of Yakima, and then pick up Hwy 97, traveling through a landscape of farmland. At Goldendale, travel 25 miles along Hwy 142–a road considered by many to be one of the most scenic in Washington. The two-lane road weaves a path through rolling farmland, at times banded by sweeps of the Klikckitat River. Should you be blessed with a clear day, you will look across to the 12,276-feet high snowcapped peak of **Mount Adam** on the Washington side, and Oregon's highest peak Mount Hood at 11,239 feet, rising impressively in the distance. The 142 delivers you to the east side of the Columbia River and Gorge, and from here, you can conveniently pick up our *Vines to Volcano* itinerary recommendation.

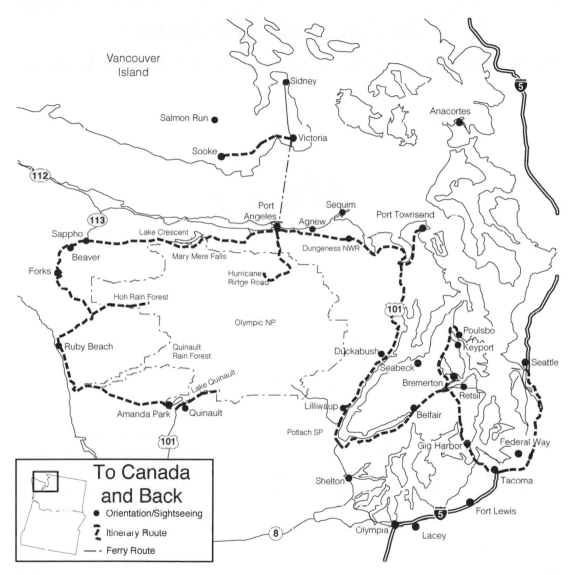

Vancouver
Island

Sidney

Salmon Run

Anacortes

Victoria

Sooke

112

113

Sequim

Port Townsend

Port
Angeles

Agnew

Sappho

Lake Crescent

Dungeness NWR

Beaver

Mary Mere Falls

Forks

Hurricane
Ridge Road

Hoh Rain Forest

Olympic NP

101

Poulsbo

Ruby Beach

Quinault
Rain Forest

Duckabush

Keyport

Seattle

Seabeck

Lake Quinault

Bremerton

Amanda Park

Quinault

Lilliwaup

Belfair

Retsil

101

Potlach SP

Gig Harbor

Federal Way

Shelton

Tacoma

Fort Lewis

5

8

Olympia

Lacey

To Canada
and Back

● Orientation/Sightseeing

Itinerary Route

- - - Ferry Route

To Canada & Back Again
Port Townsend, The Olympic Peninsula & Victoria

Victoria's Legislative Building

Once you've ventured as far as Seattle, it's easy to get to British Columbia for a peek at West Coast Canadian life. That's what we'll do in this itinerary. We'll start in Seattle and cut a not-so-usual path to Victoria—the elegant capital of British Columbia—by way of the gentle bays and inlets of southern Puget Sound, the Victorian seaport town of Port Townsend, and the majestic Olympic Peninsula. There are many ways to get to Victoria and no one way is better than another. For our purposes here, we've chosen a route that mixes things up a bit.

Recommended Pacing: Consider eight days to enjoy this itinerary. Your schedule might look like this: Spend your first travel day getting from Seattle to Port Townsend, then after one night in Port Townsend, drive to the Olympic Peninsula to explore the spectacular Olympic National Park (days 2 and 3). Next, ferry over to Victoria (day 4). Spend your first night in the city, followed by two nights in Sooke (days 5 and 6). Return to Victoria for one additional overnight (day 7), then catch a ferry back to the U.S. on the eighth day.

From Seattle, take I-5 South to Tacoma and Exit 132: Gig Harbor/Bremerton (Hwy 16). Try to avoid rush hour, and don't worry about the initial paucity of scenic wonders; we'll make it up to you soon. While this area of Puget Sound is not generally considered a holiday spot, there are several excellent bed and breakfast inns in this part of Washington nonetheless. See our recommendations in Federal Way, Tacoma, Bremerton, Seabeck, and Belfair.

Follow Hwy 16 North towards **Bremerton** (home to the Puget Sound Naval Base and the Puget Sound Naval Shipyard), then take Hwy 3 North to Route 308, where you turn right (east) to **Keyport** for a visit to the **Naval Undersea Museum**. Here you find 20,000 square feet of exhibits portraying naval history, operations, and undersea technology, with comprehensive collections including torpedoes, mines, and diving equipment; and a simulation of the control room of the nuclear fast attack submarine **Greenling**. The hands-on, Ocean Environment exhibit provides a fascinating look at the world under the sea. (610 Dowell Street: open from 10 am to 4 pm, daily in summer; closed Tuesdays in winter; 360-396-4148.)

Leaving the museum, drive west on the 308, and at the second set of traffic lights turn right on Viking Way; then, again at the second set of lights, turn right on Finn Hill Road to enter **Poulsbo**, Washington's "Little Norway," a pretty town sitting at the head of Liberty Bay. Settled in 1882 by Norwegian immigrants, Poulsbo proudly maintains its Scandinavian heritage—in the quaint downtown area you'll find the Norwegian flag and rosemaled storefronts, and you can even enjoy a traditional lutefisk dinner at the Lutheran church on the third Saturday of October. (Note: The **Marine Science Center** sadly closed due to lack of sufficient funding. One can, however, check their status through updates on their website. *www.poulsbomsc.org.*)

From Poulsbo, take Route 305 to Hwy 3 and drive south through Bremerton and Belfair, then take 106 west through Union, tracing the Hood Canal around the "Great Bend," which points you north on 101. This stretch becomes increasingly lovely as you go, where waterside residences have one terrific view.

Shortly after you reach the 101 junction, you'll pass **Potlatch State Park**. This is the site where the Skokomish and Twanoh Indian tribes once gathered for their festivals or "potlatches," ceremonies—sometimes days in length—that were held to celebrate or formalize an important event before witnesses. Just north of Potlatch but south of the town of Hoodsport (first settled in 1880), you'll happen upon the small and unassuming **Hoodsport Winery**, where local wines are available for sale. (open daily from 10 am to 6 pm; 360-877-9894; *www.hoodsport.com.*)

Winding your way closer and closer to the water's edge, you'll pass through a series of small villages with names like Lilliwaup and Duckabush, as 101 becomes increasingly more lush and forested. Clams, oysters, and shrimp are harvested from area waters here. The mighty Olympics are now stationed at your left, the peaceful waters of the Hood Canal to your right. Follow signage to Port Townsend via 20 east.

PORT TOWNSEND

A seaport town of no mean stature back in the 1800s, today's **Port Townsend** goes to heroic lengths to preserve as much of its 19th-century heritage as it can. One of only three Victorian seaport towns in the United States to earn the distinction of placement on the National Historic Register, Port Townsend and its citizens have lavished years of hard work and loving attention on its homes and neighborhoods. Visitors often come just to walk through these charming, old-world neighborhoods, soaking in the architecture and the dramatically exposed seaside setting.

The enthusiasm of this friendly and informal community, home to about 8,000 residents, will not escape you. Port Townsenders *love* to live here. They are proud of so many aspects of their community life, not the least of which is the abundance of resident and visiting artists of all disciplines who regularly present workshops, live events, and festivals. Whether it's a film festival at the **Rose Theatre** downtown or a music festival at **Centrum** in Fort Worden State Park, the creative juices are definitely flowing here. Centrum presents a very active, summer festival season; in fact, featuring blues, fiddling, jazz, and literary arts, along with chamber music, dance, and theatricals throughout the year. Phone 360-385-3102 to get hold of a schedule for the days you'll be in town.

Port Townsend is small and easy to explore; in fact, best explored on foot. Staircases guide you from the downtown area to the charming bluff side neighborhoods above. Start at the **Visitor Information Center** (open weekdays from 9 am to 5 pm; Saturdays from 10 am to 4 pm; and Sundays from 11 am to 4 pm; 888-ENJOYPT.) at 2437 Sims Way, near the waterfront and the ferry landing. From Hwy 20, you'll come after about 8 miles to a three-way stop light—turn left there onto Hwy 19 (also called Rhody Drive). Rhody becomes Sims Way. (If you are arriving by ferry from Keystone on Whidbey Island, turn left on Water Street as you exit the boat. Water Street becomes Sims Way.) Get a town map and directions to the nearby **Haines Place Park-n-Ride**. Parking is at a premium downtown and the meter maids are, shall we say, conscientious; so consider leaving your car at Haines and taking public transportation the brief distance to town and/or to Fort Worden State Park.

A must-see is the **Jefferson County Historical Society Museum**, dedicated back in 1892, which occupies the original Police Department, Court Room, City Jail, and Fire Hall. The Court Room with its original woodwork, the dramatic City Jail, and the high-ceilinged Fire Hall all contribute to a marvelous feeling of history. The museum honors the people of Jefferson County through a wonderful collection of artifacts, archives, family history, and photographs. Exhibits include *The First People: the Hoh, S'Klallam & Chimacum Tribes, The Explorers and Mariners, The Settlers and Builders*, and *The Victorians*. (540 Water Street; call for hours, which vary seasonally; 360-385-1003.)

Since this is a walking town, try an **Historical Sidewalk Tour**, led by a local historian. It makes for a great way to pass an informative hour in the waterfront district. Stories of bawdy seaport life are as entertaining as learning about the architectural landmarks. Call 360-385-1967 to make an appointment. Tours meet at the Jefferson County Historical Society Museum on Water Street. If you are interested in a guided tour of the famous bluff side neighborhoods, too, just ask.

The **Wooden Boat Foundation** at Point Hudson (380 Jefferson Street, 360-385-3628) has long made its home in Port Townsend. It's dedicated to the preservation of traditional maritime skills and culture, and offers the public a most unique outlet, the "Chandlery," that provides a ready supply of traditional boat-building materials and tools. Even if you're not personally in the market for a winch, you might take a look in the Chandlery and marvel at the "toys." Inquire here about visiting the **Northwest School of Wooden Boat Building** on the Quimper Peninsula about 4 miles south of town, if you are interested.

The **Rothschild House State Park** is a popular stop. Its historic home (Franklin & Taylor Streets, 360-379-8076) is open for self-guided tours daily from 10 am to 5 pm, May through September. Travel back in time to the 1800s as you step through the kitchen door into a home virtually unchanged since its first days. D.C.H. Rothschild, or "the Baron" as he became known locally, was born in Bavaria in 1824. After traveling extensively around the world and engaging in several business enterprises, he settled in Port Townsend in 1858 and ran a hugely successful venture devoted exclusively to the maritime trade. In 1868, he had the Rothschild House built. When he died in 1885, his widow, Dorette, decided to remain in the house and did so until her death in 1918, allowing only minimal architectural changes. Occupied only by Rothschild family members after Dorette's death, the house was donated by the last surviving relation to the Washington State Parks and Recreation Commission. The house was opened to the public in 1962 and is now listed on the National Register of Historic Places. A flower garden behind the house features many old varieties of peonies, roses, and lilacs.

Downtown and Uptown thrive as separate but distinct **shopping areas** (the former is a business district along the water and the latter a trendy residential section with a neighborhood feel), and the newer Gateway (Sims Way) now adds a third dimension.

Fort Worden State Park is easy to get to via public transportation. Otherwise, follow Cherry Street to the northern limits of Port Townsend where it meets the park. Fort Worden was once part of the defense system built to protect Puget Sound, as far back as 1896, and was in use through World War II. This is a great spot for access to the shoreline of Juan de Fuca Strait. Watch the boats go by, take a walk along the beach, or visit the **Coast Artillery Museum** (open daily, mid-May to mid-September, from 11 am to 4 pm; 360-385-4730), **Commanding Officer's House** (open daily, June to August, from 10 am to 5 pm; and from noon to 4 pm on weekends; April, May, September, and October; 360-385-4730), and **Marine Science Center** (open mid-June to mid-September from noon to 6 pm, Tuesday through Sunday; and from noon to 4 pm on weekends, April to mid-June and mid-September through October; 360-385-5582).

When you're ready, retrace your steps on Hwy 20 then head west on 101 to **Sequim** (say Skwim), long known for its dry and sunny climate—a benefit of being in the rain shadow of the Olympics. In recent years, the town has taken advantage of this Provence-style weather and is now the center of a thriving lavender industry. Visit some of the lavender fields and, if you are there in July, enjoy the vibrant Lavender Festival. There are some interesting murals in the town, but the other great attraction here is the **Dungeness National Wildlife Refuge** to the north of the town proper (reach it by going north on Kitchen Dick Road from the 101). This is the world's longest (5½ miles) natural sand spit, protecting a quiet bay that is a refuge and breeding ground for many species of native birds. You can hike out to the lighthouse at the end, and might even spot some harbor seals as well as birds.

From Sequim, we head west on the 101 to continue our Olympic Peninsula tour.

THE OLYMPIC PENINSULA

In 1897, President Grover Cleveland created the Olympic Forest Reserve in Washington State. Twelve years later, in 1909, President Theodore Roosevelt recognized a portion of this reserve as a national monument. In 1938, President Franklin D. Roosevelt signed legislation creating the **Olympic National Park**, and in 1988, nearly 95 percent of the park was designated as wilderness.

It wasn't so long ago that a trip to the Olympic Peninsula meant access to one of the most beautiful places in Washington. It meant the privilege of touching one of North America's finest, old-growth temperate rain forests. However, today as you drive along Hwy 101 you will see areas where groves of beautiful old trees have been cut indiscriminately, leaving large barren strips of land. Thankfully, the wisdom of conservationists is now prevailing and you will notice thousands of new trees being planted. Most of the clear-cutting of the forest is along the periphery of the park, and once you delve off the main road, you are in a paradise of nature that has been untouched by man.

When planning your itinerary in the Olympic National Park, you might want to consider a hotel in the nearby town of Port Angeles, since in a couple of days this is where you will be boarding the ferry to Victoria Island. However, because the scenery is so outstanding, we prefer to stay right in the heart of the park where you find a choice of delightful accommodations—not fancy hotels but simple, rustic, lodges surrounded by awesome natural splendor.

Another consideration in planning this part of your itinerary is the time of year you are traveling. Each season has its singular appeal, but for sightseeing, it is preferable to plan for the summer months when you have a better chance of sunshine. The Olympic National Park is a rain forest with an awesome amount of precipitation—the wettest months are in the winter. If you are looking for drier days, traveling in May, June, July or August offers the best chance for good weather.

It is impossible to make a loop of the Olympic National Park since there is only one main road, Hwy 101, which cuts through the park with a few smaller roads leading off to the coast or penetrating deep into pristine forests. Since there is no circular route, once you have traveled from the north end of the park to the south end, you will need to come back the same way. One suggestion would be to drive directly to the south end of the park to the Lake Quinault area and spend one night there to explore the trails. Then, the next day, return back north and spend one night near Lake Crescent to explore the trails there. If you prefer not to change hotels, just choose one as your base and take side trips each day. (Bring rain gear, by the way!)

For perspective, the drive from Lake Crescent, located on the northern end of the peninsula, to Lake Quinault, located on the southern end of the peninsula, takes about three hours, one way. You won't be able to see all the suggested sightseeing in one day, so it is best to stop at the **Olympic National Park Visitor Center** in Port Angeles. (3002 Mount Angeles Road; open from 8:30 am to 6 pm daily, June to September; and from 9 am to 4 pm daily, the rest of the year). Here you can get a map and talk to the rangers who will help you decide the best places to stop based on what most appeals to you and how much you want to hike. Follow the signage from 101 west. Get a map of the park and talk to rangers about what interests you. At the very least, you'll want to take the drive up to **Hurricane Ridge,** if weather and road conditions allow. It's well marked and only 17 miles south of the visitor center along the Heart o' the Hills/Hurricane Ridge Road. The journey up the mountain is spectacular. Watch for signs to **Lookout Rock**, a viewpoint you won't want to miss. Carrying on, you'll pass through thick forests past sub-Alpine meadows, all the way to the top of a 5,000-foot ridge. From here, if the weather is permitting, you'll see the splendid Olympic Mountains and the Pacific Ocean beyond. Look for easy **Meadow Loop Trails** that guide you through meadows covered in

Olympic National Park–Mary Mere Falls

summer with wildflowers, but bring a jacket no matter what time of year. It gets *cold* up here!

Return to 101 and drive west, passing along the southern shores of the glorious **Lake Crescent**. If you're up for a gorgeous 2-mile hike, follow the signs to the Lake Crescent Lodge (360-928-3211) and find the trailhead for the **Mary Mere Falls Trail**. This path guides you through old-growth forest to a beautiful cascade of water.

If you are keen to see something of the rain forest, continue west on 101. Pass through Sappho, Beaver, and Forks to a well marked road leading you 18 miles inland to the **Hoh Rain Forest**. The temperate rain forest in this valley (and this is true of Quinault and Queets Valleys, too) contains some of the most spectacular examples of undisturbed Sitka spruce/western hemlock forests in the U.S., where trees easily reach heights of some 300 feet. Precipitation here ranges from 12 to 14 *feet* every year! Nearly every bit of space is taken up with a living plant, as you will see. The mountains to the east prevent severe weather extremes, and very often the canopy of trees, mosses, lichen, and fern is so thick that falling snow is caught in the cover and never reaches the ground at all. Several short and easy trails will guide you through the forest.

Head out of Hoh and in the direction of 101 again. Take it south and follow signs out to the stunning **Ruby Beach** (a photographer's dream) and have a stroll along a rocky, log-strewn shore to enjoy gazing at dramatic rock formations. This is justifiably one of the most scenically distinctive beaches in this 10-mile stretch of **Kalaloch** (say CLAY a lock) **Beaches**, all considered excellent examples of primitive Pacific coastline. Beach 2 is the least rocky. Explore as you like. Watch for gray whales on their migrations from Alaska to Mexico, or for bald eagles that soar overhead or rest in the treetops on the cliffs.

Leaving the beach area that stretches south from Ruby to Beach 1, continue on 101 to North Shore Road through the **Quinault Rain Forest** onto South Shore Road for a stunning 30-mile loop around **Lake Quinault**. This loop—admittedly not well marked—crosses the Quinault River and meanders through beautifully unspoiled sections of rain forest. The road gets pretty rugged—unpaved and out-and-out rocky in sections—but if you're up for the adventure, you won't regret the trip. If you prefer to explore on foot, there are many marvelous possibilities. Begin by stopping at the ranger station situated on the side of the road on the south shore of Lake Quinault. Here you can pick up information, maps, and suggestions from the rangers about the well marked paths that weave deep into the forest. One of our favorites is the Quinault Loop Trail, which begins across the road from the Lake Quinault Lodge. Another of our favorites is the Kestner Homestead Trail that begins on the north side of the lake. Again, there is a ranger station located nearby. Stop here first to pick up a map and ask the ranger for his trail suggestions. This path winds beneath towering maple trees, traverses a sparkling creek, and passes by an abandoned homestead, once owned by early pioneers, the Kestner family (you can see their photos in the ranger station which is located where the trail begins).

Ruby Beach

VICTORIA, THE CITY OF GARDENS

Now dust off your passport. It's time to take a ferry ride across the Juan de Fuca Strait to the beautiful city of Victoria at the south end of Vancouver Island, the capital of Canada's westernmost province, British Columbia. Citizens of the U.S. visiting Canada need to supply proof of citizenship (either a valid passport, or, alternatively, a driver's license together with a copy of your birth certificate or voter's registration card).

Ferry Travel: It is important to arrive at the Port Angeles ferry terminal well ahead of your scheduled sailing time. In summer months the wait can be several hours; in which case, you'll want to leave your car in line and go off for a good meal somewhere. Local residents are the perfect sources for tips on cutting through the mystery that is ferry travel. Your innkeeper can call down to the terminal the day prior to your departure and advise you how early to arrive at the terminal. Whatever you do, plan this part ahead of time. There's nothing to spoil your trip faster than arriving at the terminal, only to find that the queue is miles long, and the next ferry is not scheduled for several more hours, or worse: the next day! Fare and seasonal schedule information are available from Washington State Ferries. If you're in Seattle, you can get timetables at their Information Desk, Colman Dock/Pier 52, between 8:15 am and 6 pm weekdays. Otherwise call 206-464-6400 (from anywhere), 511 (automated information, from Washington only), or 888-808-7977 (from Washington only), *www.wsdot.wa.gov/ferries*.

Currency: The Canadian exchange rate is so favorable to the American pocketbook, you'll have the option to stay in especially lovely places and pay only a fraction of the U.S. value. Check your local bank or our website (*www.karenbrown.com*) for the current exchange rate.

Victoria has a decidedly unique personality. It's rather small (325,000 residents) and very European (certainly British, named in 1843 for the then-recently crowned Queen of England); but also a reflection of its debt to native Coast Salish Indian, French, and—today—even Asian contributions. The mix of proud and colorful totem poles with venerable British architecture will keep you guessing, to be sure. As you approach the Inner Harbor on your ferry ride over from Port Angeles, you'll know in a delightful instant that you are about to experience a unique and wonderful place.

Very near the ferry dock at 812 Wharf Street, the **Visitor Information Centre** is a good place for gathering brochures about all the activities available to you: museums, whale-watching charters, harbor cruises, and the like. (Open from 8:30 am to 6:30 pm daily; 250-953-2033.)

When we think of Victoria, we think first of the **Royal British Columbia Museum**, surely one of the most impressive regional museums anywhere. Plan to spend several hours; it's an extraordinary place and you shouldn't miss it. Through four exceptional "galleries"—much too subtle a term—the museum showcases the human and natural history of British Columbia from prehistoric times to the present. Highly realistic and thoroughly compelling displays—not entirely unlike living museum formats—provide visitors with a very real sense of traveling back in time. Galleries are themed: First Peoples, Modern History, Natural History, and Open Oceans, all in the permanent collection. Located at the corner of Belleville and Douglas Streets, the museum is close to both the Parliament Buildings and the Empress Hotel. (Open daily from 9 am to 5 pm; 250-356-7226 or 888-447-7977, *royalbcmuseum.bc.ca*.) A **National Geographic IMAX theater** inside is also open daily, from 9 am to 8 pm.

Just east of the museum sits **Helmcken House**. Originally a three-room log house, this home was built in 1852 by Dr. John Helmcken, a surgeon with the Hudson's Bay Company, who went on to become a statesman responsible for helping to negotiate the entry of British Columbia into Canada as a province. A tour of the house reveals many original furnishings and professional belongings. Now the oldest house in British Columbia still on its original site, the house offers a fascinating glimpse into the life of Victoria long ago. (Douglas and Belleville Streets; open May to October, daily, from 10 am to 5 pm, and on Thursdays through Sundays the rest of the year.)

Take a self-guided tour (but mind you, there are nearly 100 stairs involved!) of **Craigdarroch Castle Historic House Mansion**. This impressive mansion was built between 1887 and 1890 for Scottish immigrants Robert and Joan Dunsmuir, who made their fortune from local coal. Now a national historic site, this 39-room castle features an extensive collection of stained- and leaded-glass windows, as well as magnificent woodwork. From the very top of the tower, you'll be rewarded with a gorgeous view of the city and the Olympics. (1050 Joan Crescent; open daily between June 15th and Labor Day from 9 am to 7 pm, and from 10 am to 4:30 pm the rest of the year; 250-592-5323.)

The **Parliament Buildings** at 501 Belleville Street will surely remind you of London. Victoria is the seat of the provincial government of British Columbia; and visitors are welcome to amble about these structures from June until Labor Day between 9 am and 5 pm, and between 9 am and 4 pm the rest of the year. There are also free, guided tours every hour. During assembly sessions, you may observe the proceedings from public galleries on the third floor. Lined in thousands of tiny, white lights, these buildings are particularly fetching at night. An imposing bronze likeness of Queen Victoria guards the plaza in front, and a gilt statue of Captain George Vancouver tops the central dome.

The **Empress Hotel** is a landmark in Victoria (721 Government Street; 250-384-8111). It's one of the most remarkable buildings, resembling a grand French château. Opening in 1908, the Empress earned an international reputation for its opulent guestrooms, beautiful gardens, afternoon tea service, and lavish evening entertainment. Today, many visitors throng to the Tea Lobby for a taste of history in an atmosphere of old-world sophistication and elegance. Keep in mind, however, that there are many wonderful tea rooms in Victoria, especially if you're looking for something more intimate. We have it on good authority, for example, that the **White Heather Tea Room** is a favorite among the locals. (1885 Oak Bay Avenue; open from 9:30 am to 5 pm, Tuesday to Saturday; and from 10 am to 5 pm, Sunday; 250-595-8020.) It's located east of downtown in a neighborhood called **Oak Bay**, known for its distinctly British personality, stunning Tudor-style homes, meticulous landscaping, fine shops, and . . .a proper tea service.

Consider a visit to the **Maritime Museum of British Columbia** in the Inner Harbor. The colorful story of British Columbia's marine history is told in a series of excellent theme galleries, from Early Exploration to Captain Cook, Canadian Pacific Steamships, and the Royal Navy. The stories told here are intriguing, right down to that of one John Antle, a missionary mariner who brought religion by boat to Victoria's logging camps. (28 Bastion Square; open daily from 9:30 am to 4:30 pm.)

A pleasant way to see the lovely southern and eastern shores of Victoria's waterfront communities is to take the **Scenic Marina Drive**, which starts on Dallas Road at Fisherman's Wharf Park. Drive through the James Bay residential neighborhood; through

Beacon Hill Park with its acres of gardens, lakes, and walking paths; past Ross Bay, Foul Bay, and MacNeill Bay; through the very British Oak Bay neighborhood and its Willows Beach; past Uplands Park estates; around Cadboro Bay, where the largest native village in the area once stood; past the University of Victoria; and on to Ten Mile Point.

For spectacular 360-degree views of the city, the Gulf and San Juan Islands, and the Olympic Mountains, take a drive to the top of **Mount Douglas Park** (5 miles northeast of downtown off Royal Oak and Cordova Bay Roads).

SOJOURN IN THE VILLAGE OF SOOKE

Some of the most delightful bed and breakfast inns anywhere are located in the harbor side village of **Sooke**, a 45-minute drive west on Hwy 14 from downtown Victoria. Truly, some of these inns are destination spots in themselves; and anyway, a trip to Sooke is about rest and nature, not about all there is to *do*.

Stop at the **Visitor Information Centre** at 2070 Phillips Road right off Hwy 14. Pick up maps and activity ideas (whale watching, kayaking, fresh- and salt-water fishing, hiking, gallery hopping). (Open from 9 am to 6 pm, daily in summer; and from 9 am to 5 pm, Tuesday to Sunday at all other times of year; 250-642-6351.)

For as long as anyone knows, the Coast Salish people (in particular the T'Sou-ke Nation) lived in this area, reef-netting salmon around Becher Bay and collecting shellfish, berries, and roots for winter months spent at Pedder Bay. In 1790, the rhythm of Indian life was interrupted with the arrival of Spanish explorer Manuel Quimper; then within five years, all lands north of the Strait of Juan de Fuca became British. By the 1880s, with the Hudson's Bay Company in full swing in British Columbia, East Sooke became a busy place: sailing ships and dugout canoes ran supplies to and from "Fort Victoria" and a water-powered sawmill provided lumber for the community. Loggers and fishermen sought their livelihoods here. Miners of copper and iron were plentiful.

Today, the site where many of these loggers, fishermen, and miners lived and worked is now the beautiful **East Sooke Regional Park**, offering great hiking trails along windswept rocky coastline, over rugged hilltops with panoramic views of the Olympic Peninsula, through old-growth rain forests, and into sheltered coves. The **East Sooke Coast Trail** (trailhead at Pike Road) is considered one of the best day hikes in all of Canada, a rough and strenuous, but extremely rewarding, six-hour adventure for experienced hikers. If you're looking for a hike that's not quite so ambitious, there are plenty to choose from—at Aylard Farm off Becher Road at the southeast corner of the park, at Anderson Cove off East Sooke Road on the north end of the park, or from Pike Road just off East Sooke Road at the southwest corner. Information posted at trailheads will help you choose a hike suited to your goal for the day.

Sooke Village, where most of the region's roughly 11,600 residents live, is considered the gateway to miles of unspoiled beaches, meandering rainforest trails, and gorgeous views of Sooke Harbour, the Strait of Juan de Fuca, and the Olympics.

Whiffen Spit Park, at the end of Whiffen Spit Road in the Sooke Village area, is a natural breakwater between the Juan de Fuca Strait and Sooke Harbour. A relaxing 20-minute walk to the end of the spit is a favorite among residents and visitors alike. Bird watching from the spit is especially rewarding.

You'll hear a lot in Victoria and in Sooke about the **Galloping Goose Trail**, an easy, well-paved, 35-mile (one-way) trail from the west end of the Johnson Street Bridge in Victoria to Leechtown on the Sooke River. Hikers, cyclists, and horseback riders will discover farmland, forests, seascapes, lakes, rivers, and canyons as they follow the course of the trail. But don't feel as if you have to take on the entire route to appreciate it. In the Sooke area, access points with parking lots can be found at Roche Cove on Gillespie Road, and about 1 mile up on Sooke River Road. (The trail runs right in back of **Cooper's Cove Guesthouse**.)

If you are fortunate that your trip happens in the late fall (late October to early December), I would encourage you to follow the path of the Sooke River to witness the Salmon Run. The river runs thick with the struggling fish, determined to complete their journey. Incredibly, the Chinook (or King), Coho (or Silver), Chum (or Silver Brite),

Sockeye (or Red) and Pink salmon all return, to the exact place where they spawned, to die; and, although all in the same general area, the locations are very specific. Each species is distinctive in its coloring, so visually it is easy to determine the different birthing areas. There is no dramatic staging in terms of where to go . . . just follow the river and you will notice a few key places where you can pull off, park, and there will be State Park billboards explaining the migration. The wonder of nature continues when you witness soaring bald eagles and splashing, killer whales in the bay waters—both taking advantage of easy prey. If you are brave enough to stay into the early evening, you might find yourself in the company of bears who wander down to the river's edge for a bite to eat. A memorable experience.

HOME AGAIN

When it's time to head back to Seattle, you'll ferry across the Strait of Juan de Fuca in a picturesque 2½- to 3-hour sail to **Anacortes**, Washington. Your ferry will depart from the Canadian town of **Sidney**, just north of Victoria by about 20 miles, where the Washington State Ferry system operates flexible and convenient car ferry service. Make your ferry reservation either online or by phone at least 48 hours in advance (U.S. 206-464-6400 and Canada 888-808-7977, 7 am to 6 pm.) A non-refundable deposit, applied to either your MasterCard or Visa, will be taken to confirm your reservation.

Once you're in Anacortes, the drive back to Seattle is at most an hour and a half via 20 east, then I-5 South.

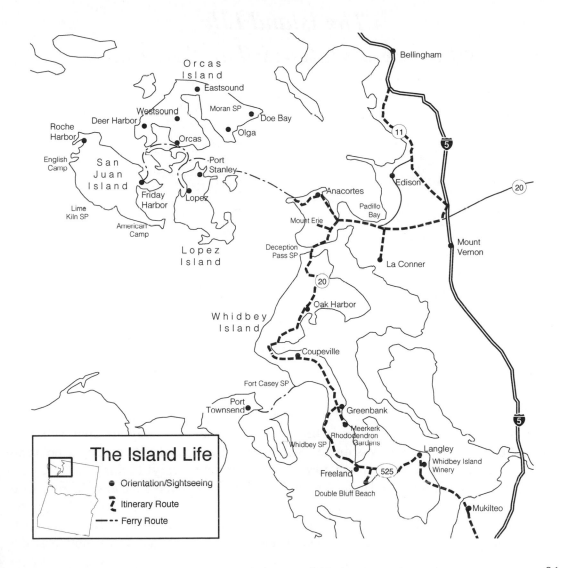

Bellingham

Orcas
Island

Eastsound

Moran SP

Westsound
Deer Harbor

Doe Bay

Roche
Harbor

Orcas

Olga

11

5

English
Camp

Port
Stanley

San
Juan
Island

20

Edison

Lime
Kiln SP

Friday
Harbor

Lopez

Anacortes

Padillo
Bay

American
Camp

Mount Erie

Mount
Vernon

Lopez
Island

Deception
Pass SP

La Conner

20

Oak Harbor

Whidbey
Island

Coupeville

Fort Casey SP

Port
Townsend

Greenbank

Meerkerk
Rhododendron
Gardens

Whidbey SP

Langley

Whidbey Island
Winery

Freeland

525

Double Bluff Beach

Mukilteo

5

The Island Life

● Orientation/Sightseeing

⌇ Itinerary Route

- - - Ferry Route

The Island Life
Whidbey, Fidalgo & The San Juans

San Juan Island–Roche Harbor

Truly ready to slow down? Good, because that's the only way to approach your exploration of the islands in Washington State; especially considering that ferry boats are in your imminent future and you are now at their charming mercy! In this itinerary, we'll downshift to "island time." Leaving Seattle far behind, we'll make the easy jaunt over to Whidbey Island, head north to Fidalgo Island, ferry hop our way through the lovely San Juans, and return to Seattle via the mainland; with a recommended side trip up to Bellingham via La Conner and the scenic Chuckanut Drive. What you'll notice is that there are many riches to explore in the north of Washington State, both on the mainland and among the islands. Our recommended routes are presented only as suggestions to get you started. You may choose to mix and match routes differently. There's no right or wrong way to explore, so follow your own heart and timeline.

Recommended Pacing: Plan on at least a two-night stay on Whidbey Island. Bunk in one spot, perhaps, and use it as a base for exploration. Since Whidbey is a very small island, getting around is easy, even if you do some backtracking in a day. Some of the best inns ever are here and you'll want time to enjoy them. We recommend at least five days to explore the San Juan Islands leisurely, especially if you want to try a kayaking or whale-watching adventure. Keep in mind, too, that the ferry schedule will make a definite impact on how you plan, so give yourself over to island life! If you have time for the picturesque detour to Bellingham on your return journey, allow half a day in La Conner, then stay overnight in La Conner or Bellingham.

WHIDBEY ISLAND

Named in about 1792 after Captain George Vancouver's sailing master, **Whidbey Island** is the largest of the Puget Sound islands. Its length from top to bottom is only 60 miles and getting to it from Seattle is easy: at most a 30-minute drive north to the ferry terminal, followed by a 20-minute crossing. We'll take you on a tour of the more interesting spots on the island as we head northward to Deception Pass, where we'll cross the Strait of Juan de Fuca onto Fidalgo Island en route to another ferry, and the first of our stops in the San Juan Islands.

From Seattle, take I-5 North to 525 North/Mukilteo. Keep left on the Mukilteo Speedway, passing signs that say 99 South/Lynwood, and continue to the Mukilteo Ferry Terminal, where you'll queue for the Whidbey Island Ferry.

Once on Whidbey, you'll first pass through the small town of **Clinton**, once a steamboat refueling spot, and today home to the busiest of Whidbey's two ferry docks. A strong Norwegian heritage influences many of the activities in Clinton and on the island generally. Drive north on 525 for 2 to 3 miles and turn right on Langley Road. Our first stop is the **Whidbey Island Vineyard and Winery,** on the right in a little less than 2 miles. Begun in 1986, the winery is owned and operated by Gregory and Elizabeth Osenbach, who proudly handcraft small lots of wine using traditional European methods. Let them introduce you to their award-winning wines: crisp, fragrant whites; an unusual and lighthearted rhubarb wine; plus serious reds and whites from classic varieties grown in eastern Washington. The Osenbachs specialize in grape varieties from the cooler parts of Europe: France's Loire Valley and Alsace, Germany, and Eastern Europe. (5237 South Langley Road; open Thursday to Sunday, from noon to 5 pm, September through June; and daily, except Tuesday, from noon to 5 pm, in July and August; 360-221-2040; *www.whidbeyislandwinery.com.*)

Leaving the winery, turn right onto Langley Road and head in the direction of the town of **Langley**. Langley Road becomes Sixth. Turn right on Anthes Avenue and drive to First. Park anywhere you like and take to this charming village on foot. Perched on a low bluff overlooking Saratoga Pass, Mount Baker, and the Cascades, Langley's lovely waterfront, historic buildings, walkways, and parks await you. This is a thriving arts community; home to many regional, national, and international artists. Browse among bookstores, bakeries, art galleries, shops, jewelers, and restaurants to your heart's content.

When you're ready to move on, drive back up Anthes and turn right on Third, heading west. Third becomes Brooks Hill Road, and from here it's a short and lovely drive out to **Double Bluff Beach**, not one of the prettiest, but certainly one of the better, beaches for collecting shells, digging up clams, and spotting bald eagles—especially during low tide. To get to Double Bluff, take Brooks Hill (which becomes Bayview Road) to 525 North and turn right. Drive 2 miles and turn left on Double Bluff Road. The road ends at the beach. See if you can spot an eagle in search of its next meal out over the water.

Retrace your steps back to 525 North and turn left. Turn left again on Bush Point Road (which will eventually become Smuggler's Cove Road) and drive 6 miles to **South Whidbey State Park** (360-331-4559). Here you have a handful of short trails to choose from, whether through old-growth forest or out to the beach. All are easy, ranging from almost standing in place to a gentle loop of almost 2 miles—a very tranquil spot.

Leaving the park, turn left on Smuggler's Cove and head initially in the direction of Coupeville. When you get to 525, however, make a right turn and head south. We're going to backtrack for a moment. Turn left at the signs to **Greenbank Farm** (open daily from 10 am to 5 pm; 360-678-7700), an unassuming and thoroughly welcoming place that has become an island landmark over the years. In the early 1900s, the Philips family wondered what the land on Whidbey Island would grow. After much in the way of experimentation, they switched in the 1930s from dairy to berry farming, and by 1972 the Greenbank Berry Farm was known as the largest loganberry farm in the United States. When that way of life was threatened in recent years by possible development of the farm's 522 acres, an intense local effort resulted in the acquisition of the farm by the citizens of the island in 1997. Browse through the gift shop, buy some loganberry jam, taste one of the many fine wines of the Puget Sound Appellation, or enjoy a light lunch or snack (with a delicious slice of pie, of course!) in the Whidbey Pies Café. The locals who run the place are incredibly friendly. Many activities are scheduled year round at the farm, including a **Sunday Market,** each Sunday from mid-May to October, when you can buy island-grown produce, flowers, and crafts from 11 am to 2 pm. In July, the farm celebrates its agricultural heritage with the annual **Loganberry Festival**. August brings the skirl of bagpipes and the swirl of kilts at the **Highland Games**, while in December, **Winter on Whidbey** means hayrides, bonfires, hot cider, and caroling.

Return to 525 and continue south to **Meerkerk Rhododendron Gardens,** only 3 miles down the road. Turn left on Resort Road, then left again onto Meerkerk Lane, following signs to the gardens. For a small admission fee, spend an hour or more strolling through these beautiful grounds, home to more than 2,000 rhododendrons, but also to 43 acres of gorgeous forests. Take the **Harborside Trail** to the parkside cliffs and watch for whales and bald eagles. Special events are scheduled year round in the gardens, including the **Whidbey Island Folk Music Festival** on the first weekend in August and a **Mother's**

Day Concert on the second Sunday in May. (Open daily from 9 am to 4 pm, with the spring blooming season best between March and May; 360-678-1912.)

Make your way back again to 525 and this time head north. Take 20 west in the direction of the Port Townsend Ferry. You can make a day trip to Port Townsend (we cover the town in another itinerary) or follow the frontage road past the ferry terminal to **Fort Casey State Park** (open daily from 8 am until sundown; 360-678-4519). Here at Admiralty Head, Fort Casey was built in the 19th century as part of a larger defense system designed to protect the entrance to Admiralty Inlet. No guns were actually fired from this spot, but the fort was used as a training location during both World Wars. The **Admiralty Head Lighthouse** has been transformed into an interpretive center on the fort's history and is open from 11 am to 5 pm, Wednesday to Sunday and on holidays.

Leaving Fort Casey, follow the signs to Engle Road and **Coupeville**. The oldest of Whidbey Island's towns, Coupeville was first established in 1853. Brochures for self-guided walking tours through this 19th-century seaport town are available at the **Island County Historical Museum**, a good place to begin. A brief video in the museum will introduce you to the area's history. (908 N. Alexander Street at the corner of Front; open daily, May to September, from 10 am to 5 pm; 360-678-3310.) You'll also learn about **Ebey's Landing National Historic Reserve**, 17,400 acres of remarkable prairie land, thoughtfully preserved so that future generations might appreciate the cultural and geographic heritage of this once-bustling farming and seafaring community. Ask in the museum for directions to the 1-mile trail from the beach at Ebey's Landing (at the foot of Ebey Road) to **Sunnyside Cemetery** at Cook and Sherman Roads. The cemetery contains the headstones of some of the region's pioneer families. From it, you'll have marvelous views of the prairie and the water. Meanwhile, stroll the streets of town and try to imagine what it might have been like over 150 years ago when the first European settlers arrived at this home of the Coast Salish Indians.

Don't return from Coupeville to Hwy 20 just yet. Instead, take **Madrona Way** (west of Broadway) from town. It's a scenic 4-mile frontage road that guides you along Penn

Cove and connects to Hwy 20 a bit farther north. Once back on 20, drive straight through Oak Harbor, home to the Whidbey Island Naval Air Station, and on to Deception Pass.

The beautiful **Deception Pass State Park** (360-675-2417) includes not only this northernmost tip of Whidbey Island, but also the area of Fidalgo Island just across the dramatic Deception Pass Bridge. It represents a total of over 4,000 acres of protected shoreline, land, and trails. Rocky, driftwood-strewn beaches here are popular for day-trippers who come to revel in the sunsets seen across Rosario Strait from Bowman Bay (on the north side of the bridge). You might want to enjoy one of the hiking trails in the park, some of which guide you into groves of tall trees, while others take you along lakes or coastline. Find a park map and see what calls to you. On the north side of the bridge, for example, is a short 4/5-mile loop around **Rosario Head**. Follow the Rosario Beach signs once you've crossed the bridge, leave your car in the parking lot, and look for signage to the **Rosario Head Trail**. From the vista point midway along the trail, you'll gaze in awe across the water and back over to Whidbey.

Once you are ready to leave Whidbey to continue our tour to the San Juans, cross Deception Pass Bridge and continue north in the direction of Anacortes, taking a detour to **Mount Erie**. Well marked from the highway, a steep, meandering road will lead you, up and up, to the top of this 1,273-foot mountain for sweeping views in all directions of Puget Sound, Mount Baker, the North Cascade range, and—weather cooperating—Mount Rainier. In springtime, you'll find the valley's gorgeous tulip and daffodil fields mesmerizing from this vantage point, as you will the opportunity to watch bald eagles fly *beneath* you for a change. Continue north and west on 20 to Anacortes and the Washington State Ferry terminus. It's time to introduce you to the San Juan Islands.

THE SAN JUAN ISLANDS

So much has already been written about the **San Juans**, that tranquil chain of Washington islands (hundreds of them!) that in fact are the tops of a submerged mountain range. Visitors come here to sail, kayak, bicycle, whale watch, bird watch, nap, and just generally slow down. As many as 40 of the San Juan Islands are said to be inhabited, but only four of them are serviced by commercial ferry. Of these four, only three offer accommodations: San Juan Island, Orcas Island, and Lopez Island. Ah, and what accommodations: some of the best in all of Washington!

Ferry Travel: Washington State Ferries make multiple, daily departures to all the islands we cover in this itinerary. These ferries provide inter-island service for vehicles and foot or bicycle passengers alike. Since reservations are not accepted, it is important to arrive at any terminal at **least** one hour ahead of your scheduled sailing time. Longer waits are possible at peak travel times (e.g., summer and holiday weekends). Local residents are the perfect source for tips on cutting through the mystery that is ferry travel. Your innkeeper can call down to the terminal on the day prior to or the day of your departure, and advise you how early to arrive at the terminal depending on traffic that day. Whatever you do, *ask*. There's nothing to spoil your trip faster than arriving at a terminal, only to find that the queue is miles long and the next ferry not scheduled for several more hours!

Fare and seasonal schedule information are available from **Washington State Ferries**. If you're in Seattle, you can get timetables at their Information Desk, Colman Dock/Pier 52, between 8:15 am and 6 pm weekdays. Otherwise call 206-464-6400 (from anywhere), 511 (automated information, from Washington only), or 888-808-7977 (from Washington only). Or visit *www.wsdot.wa.gov/ferries*.

Bicycling: Many visitors venture to the San Juans to bicycle. Lopez, where roads traverse pastoral landscapes and provide sweeping mountain and water views, has relatively flat terrain and is the easiest to tour on two wheels. The village is only about 4 miles from the ferry landing. Orcas is the most challenging, especially for those hardy bodies who brave the 5 vertical miles to the summit of Mount Constitution. Eastsound is located mid-island on Orcas; it's a good spot for stocking up on water and refreshments. San Juan combines flatlands and hills with a good variety of scenic destinations. Stock up in Friday Harbor or Roche Harbor. Most roads are narrow and winding with shoulders that range from barely adequate to non-existent. Wear a helmet, travel single file in small groups, and pull well out of the way if you need to stop along the road, especially near a ferry landing where traffic is most concentrated.

Golf: Private, nine-hole, courses are open to the public for modest green fees. All offer club and cart rentals.

Lopez Golf Club	360-468-2679
Orcas Golf Club	360-376-4400
San Juan Golf Club	360-378-2254

Kayaking: If you are kayaking on your own, it's important to understand the location of ferry and shipping lanes, and the ever-changing tides and currents. Guidelines are available at the Whale Museum in Friday Harbor on San Juan Island (see next page).

Whale Watching: Scheduled whale- and wildlife-watching trips are offered from May to October. The Whale Museum, in Friday Harbor on San Juan Island (see next page for details), offers the best information about tours and the resident orca population. You can view a list of **Whale Watch Operators Association NW** members on their website, *www.nwwhalewatchers.org/members.html.*

Weather Wise: The San Juan Islands get about half the amount of rain that Seattle gets. Summer temperatures range between 65 and 80 degrees Fahrenheit. At other times, don sweatshirts and sweaters when temperatures range between 40 and 60 degrees Fahrenheit. Fall and winter are considered rainy seasons but the sun is often out nonetheless.

Ready then? Get a ferry schedule and plot your island hopping anyway you please. We'll start at the last stop on the ferry route, on the second-largest and most-populated island: San Juan.

SAN JUAN ISLAND

San Juan Island, once home to fruit growers and farmers, is today the busiest and most populated of all the San Juans. Because it covers only 55 square miles, driving the entire island in a day is entirely doable; but you'll want to move at a slower pace so you can linger as you go. Here are some of the highlights, listed roughly in a clockwise direction from **Friday Harbor**, the island's primary commercial center, home to just over 2,000 residents; and the hub for restaurants, small museums, shops, galleries, and parks.

Now that you are in prime orca territory, **The Whale Museum** is a delightful must, not because it's elaborate, but because it offers an informative and heartfelt presentation designed to educate us about whales and the marine ecosystem upon which they depend for survival. This the best place to inquire about whale-watching tours. (62 First Street N in Friday Harbor; open daily from 9 am to 5 pm, Memorial Day to Labor Day, and from 10 am to 5 pm the rest of the year; 360-378-4710 or 800-946-7227; *www.whale-museum.org*.)

The **San Juan Historical Museum** holds the unique title of "most northwestern museum in the continental United States." Located on the homestead of early settler James King, it is actually a small complex of island buildings, some of which have been relocated to this spot. See an original farmhouse, the first county jail, a 19th-century log cabin, a barn, a milk house, and a carriage house. You'll appreciate the museum if you are keen to know more about local history, or if you happen to be tracing your genealogy back to the islands. (405 Price Street in Friday Harbor; open Tuesday and Thursday, from 10 am to 2 pm, October to April; and Thursday to Saturday, from 1 to 4 pm, May to September; 360-378-3949.)

American Camp (**San Juan Island National Historic Park**) at the most southeastern point on the island was the American military settlement during the "Pig War" of 1859–72. At the time, there was considerable disagreement about who owned the San Juan Islands: was it the U.S. or Britain? Tensions came to a head in 1859, when an American farmer shot a pig rooting uninvited in his potato patch. As it turned out, the pig belonged to the very British Hudson's Bay Company. Believe it or not, the U.S. Infantry was dispatched to San Juan Island, as were several British warships. After an initial standoff involving no fighting, joint occupation was agreed upon and lasted until 1872, when Kaiser Wilhelm of Germany, invited to serve as arbiter, decided in favor of the Americans.

Today, American Camp is headquarters to the island's National Historic Park. In a building at the entrance, you can view a brief slide show about the Pig War and pick up a brochure for a self-guided walking tour of the grounds. Several original structures still stand, including a campsite and an officers' quarters. Along Griffin Bay to the north, a trail guides you through woods above several lagoons. From the trail, you'll see beautiful broad beaches, and perhaps, a pod of orcas making its seasonal migration.

Easily one of the loveliest spots on the island is the drive along **West Side Road**. Take it to the tiny **Lime Kiln Point State Park**, perhaps better known now as **Whale Watching Park**. Poised along De Haro Strait, this section of parkside water is known to be a favorite cruising spot for pods of orcas and minkes who spend their summers in these waters. Park the car and walk along the cliffs and by the tidepools. You are likelier to see whales in summer months, if you time your visit for late afternoon/early evening. This is the time of year when most sightings are documented. The **Lime Kiln Lighthouse** is now a whale research station. It uses underwater microphones to monitor and study the communications between whales.

Near the northwestern corner of the island, just off W. Valley Road, you'll discover **English Camp (San Juan Island National Historic Park)**, the other side of the Pig War story. Here you'll be able to wander past a handful of clapboard buildings and even a formal British garden overlooking Garrison Bay. In the **Barracks**, photographs tell the story of the early days of the conflict. Check out the **English Camp Cemetery**, where soldiers, who thankfully never had to fight, lie buried. (Open daily from dawn to dusk.)

Roche Harbor at the north end of the island now stands on the spot first occupied by a Hudson's Bay Company post. When the U.S./Canadian boundary was settled, it became the Roche Harbor Lime Quarries and changed hands several times until it was purchased by John McMillan in 1886. McMillan was responsible for making this harbor a key port of entry, complete with customs office, and managed what became the largest lime production company in the entire Northwest. It's that sense of history that brings visitors to this bustling resort community today; with its tailored lawns, cobblestone waterfront, historic hotel, restaurants, and shops.

The relatively new **San Juan Vineyards** will be fun to watch as it grows. The only commercial vineyard and winery on the island, it was established in 1996 by three island friends with a dream. The very first harvest was in October of 2000, but it yielded unexpectedly little due to the many island birds who got to the fruit first! Hence, only a very limited bottling of its first estate wine, Madeleine Angevine, was made available in June of 2001. A netting system was installed to protect the 2001 crop, with very successful results. Consider stopping by the vineyard to see how they're doing and report back. A tasting room and gift shop occupy what was Schoolhouse Number 22 on the property, originally built in 1896. (2000 Roche Harbor Road; open from noon to 6 pm seasonally; 360-378-WINE; *www.sanjuanvineyards.com.*)

ORCAS ISLAND

Next stop, our personal favorite: **Orcas Island**. The largest (57 square miles), hilliest, and most forested of the islands, Orcas boasts the kind of terrain that may put you in mind of Ireland or Norway in many spots. The combination of greenery and water here is stunning! Once excellent shell-fishing grounds for the Lummi Indians in summer months, Orcas is home now to a population of about 4,500. We've assembled some ideas for things to do while you're on Orcas.

The commercial center is **Eastsound** to the north, a charming place for browsing through small shops, sampling good restaurants, and learning more about the island. It's a very small village, so it's easy to walk around. You may happen upon something that piques your interest, including information on biplane trips, kayaking, and whale watching. Every Saturday from May through September, enjoy the **Orcas Farmers Market** off North Beach Road, a great way to meet the locals and to sample their produce and crafts.

Rent a bike at **Dolphin Bay Bicycles,** adjacent the ferry landing. They've got a full-service bicycle shop and can give you tips for touring. (360-376-4157.)

Moran State Park is the fourth-largest park in all of Washington State. Totaling over 5,000 acres, it offers about 30 miles of trails, five lakes, beautiful forests of old-growth Douglas fir and cedar, and the highest point in the San Juan Islands: the 2,407-foot **Mount Constitution**. Take a drive up to the top of the mountain for marvelous views in all directions of the San Juans, Vancouver Island, and the Cascade and Olympic mountain ranges. Try the half-mile **Cascade Falls Trail** or the 4-mile **Mountain Lake Loop Trail**.

As you drive along Orcas Road on the west side of the island, keep a watch overhead as you go. Local sculptor Anthony Howe has hung his copper and stainless-steel art sculptures in the trees near the turnoff to his **Howe Art Gallery & Kinetic Sculpture Garden** and it makes for a magical touch (¼ mile west of Eastsound on the Horseshoe Highway; hours vary; *www.howeart.net*).

A visit to **Rosario Resort** (1 Rosario Way; 800-562-8820; *www.rosario.rockresorts.com*) on the east side of the island proves an intriguing diversion. Shipbuilding magnate Robert Moran moved to Orcas Island when, at 46 years of age, his doctor told him he had little time left to live. Moran built a mansion he named Rosario (completed in 1909), and was so rejuvenated by the whole experience that he lived another 30 years. Admire the elegant and elaborate **Moran Mansion**, the focal point of today's resort. The foundation for the mansion is cut 16 feet into solid rock, walls are made of concrete and lined inside with mahogany, windows are just shy of an inch thick, and the roof is covered with 6 tons of copper sheeting. You'd think Moran was building one of his ocean liners! Local musician Christopher Peacock performs weekly in a wonderful and informal concert in the vaulted **Music Room** on an enormous 1,972-pipe Aeolian organ. It's a fun show, in which Peacock interjects bits about the house and its original owner. The room is beautiful with its Tiffany chandelier and stained-glass windows. The private living quarters of the Moran family have been transformed into a museum, with Moran's own photographs of nature and family life lining the walls. Check out the **Spa by the Bay**. You don't have to be a guest of the hotel to enjoy their services. Restaurants are available from an informal café to fine dining.

LOPEZ ISLAND

On to **Lopez Island**, at one time referred to as "the Guernsey Island" for its exports of cream, eggs, and poultry. While most of the dairy farms have disappeared, Lopez is still very much agricultural in feel. Home to craftspeople, musicians, farmers, fishers, nature lovers, and eccentrics, Lopez maintains its long-standing custom of waving to passersby. Wander the rural roads in peace and quiet, where woods mix with farmland and tranquil water vistas. The island covers an area of less than 30 square miles and its population numbers only about 2,100.

Visitors come to Lopez not for action, but to kayak, to bicycle (the terrain is pretty flat), or to wander back roads and scan the rugged coastlines in search of wildlife. It is possible to rent bikes and kayaks locally.

The tiny village of **Lopez**, just 4 miles south of the ferry landing on Weeks Road, provides the only sign of commercial life with a few shops, a bakery, and restaurants. The humble **Lopez Historical Museum** in the village chronicles Indian and pioneer life on the island over the years (call for hours: 360-468-2049).

At **Shark Reef Sanctuary** (Shark Reef and Burt Roads to the southwest), a 1/5-mile trail through thick, old-growth forest, leads to dramatic cliffs for some excellent island and marine-life views. Visit **Lopez Island Vineyards** (724 Fisherman Bay Road; call for hours: 360-468-3644), San Juan County's oldest winery, producing organically grown grapes and fine wines. **Agate Beach** is a tiny, pebble-strewn cove well suited to taking a sunset stroll.

SHAW ISLAND

You may have heard about the friendly Franciscan nuns who operate the ferry landing on the otherwise elusive **Shaw Island**. Actually, this smallest of four islands, served by the ferry system, is home to *three* Catholic religious orders, all of them for women: the Franciscans, the Sisters of Mercy, and the Benedictines. In total, there are only about 150 residents who occupy the 5,000 forested acres of this fiercely private place. There is no commercialism of any kind on Shaw: no bed and breakfast inns, no shops, no restaurants, no mail delivery service even—and that's the way the residents like it. Volunteers run the privately endowed—and marvelous—library, the historical society, and the fire department. Many residents have to purchase their water and have it ferried in from neighboring islands!

There are really only a very few things to do on Shaw, so consider this when deciding if you want to venture over. You might want to put a bicycle on the ferry and head over for a brief visit that way. Visit the **Little Portion Store** at the ferry landing (open while the ferries are operating). Run by Franciscan nuns, this rustic store is stocked, in addition to the usual items, with a good selection of wines and handcrafted wonders made on the island, including herbal vinegars, teas, spices, Mother Prisca's Hot Mustard (made by the Benedictine nuns at Our Lady of the Rock Priory), and llama droppings for fertilizer! Inquire in the store about a possible visit to the chapel at **Our Lady of the Rock Priory**. You'll be given a phone number to call, and if the timing is right, you might be fortunate enough to be welcomed over for a visit. The **Shaw Island Historical Museum** on Blind Bay Road (ask a nun in the Little Portion Store for an island map) is located about 2 miles from the ferry landing. It's very small and rustic, constructed with logs from the original post office, and features items reflecting its proud and quiet history. (Open Tuesday from 2 to 4 pm; Thursday from 11 am to 1 pm; and Saturday from 10 am to noon and from 2 to 4 pm.) The adjacent lending library is excellent. Local residents have amassed an impressive collection of books, and anyone is welcome to browse the shelves. Only **Shaw Island State Park** at Indian Cove offers picnic tables and primitive campsites, and the spot is spectacular if your needs are few. Take all "No Trespassing" signs seriously.

BACK TO SEATTLE VIA CHUCKANUT DRIVE

Once your island visits are complete and you've exited the ferry at Anacortes, head east on Hwy 20 and follow the signs to the town of **La Conner**. On the National Register of Historic Places, this small town dates back to the late 1860s and is perhaps best known for its annual **Tulip Festival** in April, when a true profusion of tulips and daffodils are out in force. Farmland washed in spring color is a beautiful sight! Stroll the streets to enjoy the shops and restaurants, or visit the excellent **Museum of Northwest Art**. This museum showcases a small but outstanding selection of Northwest contemporary art, including a wonderful glass gallery and works by the mid-20th-century artists credited with envisioning the Northwest style: Guy Anderson, Kenneth Callahan, Morris Graves, and Mark Tobey. (121 South 1st Street; open Tuesday to Sunday from 10 am to 5 pm; 360-466-4446; *www.museumofnwart.org*.)

Return to Hwy 20 and travel west through scenic farmland; then turn north following Bayview Edison Road as it shadows the coastline and intersects with Hwy 11, otherwise known as the **Chuckanut Drive**. Park just off the road where you see signs for **Padilla Bay**, a national reserve, interpretive center and state park (360-428-1558, *www.padillabay.gov*), walk an elevated trail along a dike across the nation's largest wetland bay, and enjoy the company of hawks, bald eagles, herons, snow geese, trumpeter swans and the occasional sea otter. (For a birding map, call 360-428-8547.) Just past Edison, a town that dates back to the 1800s, turn onto Chuckanut Drive, considered one of the most scenic roads in Washington State and a great alternative to the interstate. From 1913 to 1931, this road was part of the Pacific Highway connecting Vancouver, B.C. to San Diego, California. (If time is short, take Hwy 20 east and take it to I-5 North. Exit I-5 as soon as you see signs to Hwy 11.)

The views of Puget Sound, the San Juan Islands, and the Olympic Mountains are marvelous, as you wend your way along this lush path cut into the rocky hillside to Bellingham. Take advantage of the turnouts for some spectacular views. Let yourself be tempted on roads that wind the short distance down to the water's edge to enjoy the beautiful coves, inlets, and emerald waters explored often by kayaks. There are also numerous parks whose trails wend their way up the rocky hillside and down through lush foliage. The sandy shores are prime for shellfish, and there are a few restaurants where you can stop to enjoy the view and sample the local seafood. You can also purchase oysters and crabs direct from the fisherman, as well as watch a video that teaches about oyster and clamming. Turn off Chuckanut Drive at the sign for **Taylor Shellfish Farm**. They even provide picnic tables and barbecues (charcoal is available for purchase) should you want to barbeque your own. (Open 7 days, 2182 Chuckanut Drive, 360-766-6002). The soft light of both early morning and evening are ideal for traveling this memorable route.

Bellingham is a merger of what were once four different districts, each with their own character: the port where the transport of lumber still dominates the piers, the old town, the lovely residential district that encircles the waters of Lake Whatcom, and the quaint community of Fairhaven. A favorite of ours, the **Fairhaven Historic District,** between 13th and 20th Streets just south of downtown, is good for a self-guided, walking tour. Lovingly restored brick storefronts from the 1890s now mark buildings that house cafés, restaurants, shops, and galleries in an understated, informal atmosphere. Bellingham is also home to **Western Washington University**, well known in the area for its **outdoor sculpture collection**, arranged across some 190 acres of campus grounds. Also popular in town is the **Whatcom Museum of History & Art**, devoted to regional culture and art. Bird enthusiasts love the extensive bird exhibit featuring many winged creatures common to the Northwest, while children delight in their very own hands-on museum offering stimulating exhibits and workshops. (121 Prospect Street; open Tuesday to Sunday, from noon to 5 pm, except holidays; 360-676-6981; *www.whatcommuseum.org*.)

From Bellingham it's only an 87-mile drive south on I-5 back to The Emerald City (Seattle).

Places to Stay
Vancouver Island, Canada

Get a small group of your best friends together and book a couple of nights at Cooper's Cove Guesthouse. Don't plan to leave the premises, except to hike to the beach from out the back door (access to the 40-mile Galloping Goose Trail is only a staircase away). Angelo and Ina have created a casually elegant package deal here: dinner and wonderful rooms with beautiful water views. You don't have to book dinner; but you'll want to, at least for one night. Angelo is your personal chef, has a published cookbook, and come dinnertime, you'll join him in his large, sky-lit kitchen and take a high seat at a granite-top counter to watch him at work. Bring your own bottles of wine (no liquor license here) and enjoy watching the creation of your meal. It's like going to a friend's—a friend who's a gourmet cook, for a great dinner: casual, comfortable, informal, informative, and just plain fun. Guestrooms downstairs are bright, modern, clean, and well-appointed with subtly artistic touches in unexpected places. All have king or queen beds with goose-down duvets, fireplaces, water views, private bathrooms and a balcony. Three have access to a shared hot tub; one has a private hot tub. Sherry trays and homemade truffles are delivered to your room. Whether with a group of friends or on your own, Cooper's Cove is a great, out-of-the-ordinary destination spot. *Directions:* From Victoria, take Hwy 14 west for about 35 miles. Look for a sign on your left right off the highway.

COOPER'S COVE GUESTHOUSE
Innkeepers: Angelo Prosperi-Porta & Ina Haegemann
5301 Sooke Road
Sooke, British Columbia V0S 1N0, Canada
Tel: (250) 642-5727, Fax: (250) 642-5749
Toll Free: (877) 642-5727
4 Rooms, Double: $165–$215
Dinners available
Closed: January, Credit cards: MC, VS
www.karenbrown.com/coopers.html

It's a challenge indeed to describe Richview, somehow at once: Switzerland, New Mexico, and Japan. One thing is certain, Richview has one of the most unique water views in Sooke, poised due south near an 80-foot drop into the Strait of Juan de Fuca. Simplicity of line is the hallmark in each suite, the work of François Gething's loving craftsmanship as a fine carpenter: futon-style bed frames of alder, red cedar window sills covered in cream-colored Roman shades, handsome sinks lined in eastern cherry with matching mirror frames. High vaulted-ceilings, skylights, and large windows grace these open and modestly appointed spaces. Walls are painted white and resemble adobe with their gently rounded corners. Color is used sparingly. All rooms have separate sitting areas with beautiful, wood-burning fireplaces made of stone, gorgeous water views, and small patios. In The Garden Room, a two-person jetted soaker tub as well as a two-person shower that doubles as a steam bath are beautifully crafted to take full advantage of the room's water view. Both the Spoon Room and the Frog Room have two-person soaking tubs on a protected balcony overlooking a lush garden and the ocean. This hidden and tranquil retreat is only a three-minute walk from the best restaurant in town. *Directions:* From Victoria, take Hwy 14 west through Sooke's business district. Turn left on Whiffen Spit Road and right on Richview Drive.

RICHVIEW HOUSE BY THE SEA
Innkeepers: François & Joan Gething
7031 Richview Drive
Sooke, British Columbia V0S 1N0, Canada
Tel: (250) 642-5520, Fax: (250) 642-5501
Toll Free: (866) 276-2480
3 Rooms, Double: $225
Open: all year, Credit cards: MC, VS
www.karenbrown.com/richview.html

A trip to Sooke Harbour House is a journey to Alice's Wonderland, where the impossible is, in fact, very naturally possible. Each guestroom is its own story, its own brand of magic brought to life by local craftsmen, painters, potters, and wizards making visible the dream life of Sinclair and Frederique Philip: beautiful mosaic work in gravel paths that wend through storybook gardens, set along the crashing shore; authentic Island Indian totems and ceremonial pieces, so large you'll think you've eaten the cake labeled "Eat Me" and have shrunk to a fraction of your former size; a stained-glass shower designed in joyous, floral patterns to reflect the garden outside; a delicate piece of pastel silk to cover the window and flow in the breeze. There's a chandelier in the bathroom; there are buttons on the bed cover. The headboard's a tree and the sink's not a sink but a mixing bowl. No two rooms are alike, but each is fanciful perfection. All come with a wood-burning fireplace, an endless supply of kindling, and a soul-stirring view of the water (save one). Breakfast is delivered to your door whenever you want it. One of the best restaurants in Canada is right downstairs. Sooke Harbour House is private, playful, elegant, intimate, imaginative, intelligent, and sophisticated. To top it all off wonderful massages are available. *Directions:* From Victoria, take Hwy 14 west through Sooke's business area, turn left on Whiffen Spit Road, and the inn is on the right near the water.

SOOKE HARBOUR HOUSE
Innkeepers: Sinclair & Frederique Philip
1528 Whiffen Spit Road
Sooke, British Columbia V0S 1N0, Canada
Tel: (250) 642-3421, Fax: (250) 642 6988
Toll Free: (800) 889-9688
28 Rooms, Double: $275–$575
Open: all year, Credit cards: MC, VS
Select Registry
www.karenbrown.com/sookeharbour.html

Paul and Elizabeth Kelly take justifiable pride in the outcome of their meticulous restoration work on this beautiful Victorian mansion built in 1901. The home's common rooms are particularly gorgeous: notice the bay windows in leaded stained glass, the beautiful moldings, and the handsome chandeliers. You have your pick of seven guestrooms upstairs, each decorated in Victorian style. While not the least bit overwrought, they are decidedly formal in tone. The fabrics, the wallpaper, the paint, the furniture—everything looks fresh from the shop. Rooms are bright and pleasant and vary in size to suit your needs. Tubs are stenciled and glazed by hand to match the wallpaper. Linens are top of the line. The stained-glass work you admire downstairs is found throughout the hallways and guestrooms as well, making for a very elegant touch. All rooms are uniquely decorated and most have Jacuzzi tubs. There are also two two-bedroom suites that can accommodate up to four persons. Afternoon sherry is served in the drawing room. The Haterleigh Heritage is justifiably proud of their 5 star rating by Tourism British Columbia. *Directions:* Take Government Street east. Turn right on Belleville and left on Pendray—the inn is at the junction of Kingston and Pendray; just two blocks from the city center.

A HATERLEIGH HERITAGE INN
Innkeepers: Paul & Elizabeth Kelly
243 Kingston Street
Victoria, British Columbia V8V 1V5, Canada
Tel: (250) 384-9995, Fax: (250) 384-1935
Toll Free: (866) 234-2244
7 Rooms, Double: $167–$265
Open: all year, Credit cards: MC, VS
www.karenbrown.com/haterleigh.html

Constructed in the 1930s as an eight-suite luxury apartment complex, Abigail's Hotel is an excellent choice for its quality accommodations and convenient neighborhood location, three blocks from Victoria's beautiful Inner Harbour. The exterior is quite beautiful, almost whimsically so, mixing Edwardian and Tudor influences. On the inside, you'll find a charming blend of the European and the Arts and Crafts, all put together with reserve and tailored elegance. There are three levels in the main building, accessed by stairs, and two in a newer adjacent building, The Coach House. Rooms of varying sizes are available. The newer rooms offer a few more contemporary touches, such as dark-wood plantation shutters and leather couches. Many rooms have wood burning fireplaces and Jacuzzi tubs. All rooms feature comfortable beds and luxurious linens and goose-down duvets, traditional marble bathrooms. A gourmet breakfast is available in any one of the several rooms downstairs; the sunny dining room, the library, or the patio in better weather. Wine and appetizers are served every evening in the library. The Pearl is a new spa treatment center. There's a small shop next to the reception desk for incidentals like film, bottled water, and postcards. The staff is friendly, professional, and available 24 hours a day. *Directions:* From the wharf, head east to Vancouver Street, then turn west on McClure. Guest parking is available at the back of the building.

※ ■ ☕ CREDIT ☎ 🐕 Y P ❀ ⚓ ☂ 👤 🎿 🐎 ⚓ 🍷

ABIGAIL'S HOTEL
Innkeepers: Ellen & Russ Cmolik
906 McClure Street
Victoria, British Columbia V8V 3E7, Canada
Tel: (250) 388-5363, Fax: (250) 388-7787
Toll Free: (800) 561-6565
23 Rooms, Double: $209–$450
Open: all year, Credit cards: all major
Select Registry
www.karenbrown.com/abigails.html

Andersen House is at once homey, yet sophisticated; historic, yet thoroughly modern. This 1891 Victorian has been beautifully restored and given a completely contemporary feel—open and light, and very welcoming. We admired the original art throughout the common rooms downstairs, which suit the large wall spaces very well and give the rooms a polished touch. Our favorite of the downstairs rooms is the casual, spacious dining room, with large windows and French doors that invite in the morning sun. Guestrooms are handsomely decorated in subtly stylish ways that complement the 19th-century architecture. The Garden Studio, just below ground level, is perhaps the most romantic in soft shades of pale green and white. It has low ceilings, but a lot of light through gorgeous, stained-glass windows overlooking the back garden. It has a private entrance, double Jacuzzi tub, hardwood floors, and pedestal sink right in the bedroom; plus the tiniest water closet you've ever seen. Upstairs are two very large, comfortable rooms. Casablanca has a sun deck, a Jacuzzi tub, a sitting area, and original, wood-paneled walls painted in a lovely pale yellow. The largest room, The Captain's Apartment includes a mini-kitchen, a king bed, plus two twins tucked in an alcove, and a huge bathroom with a Jacuzzi tub and two-person shower. *Directions:* Take Government Street south. Turn right on Belleville, left on Oswego, and right on Kingston.

ANDERSEN HOUSE BED AND BREAKFAST
Owners: Max & Janet Andersen
Innkeeper: Richard Jefferson
301 Kingston Street
Victoria, British Columbia V8V 1V5, Canada
Tel: (250) 388-4565, Fax: (250) 721-3938
Toll Free: (877) 264-9988
4 Rooms, Double: $195–$275
Open: all year, Credit cards: MC, VS
www.karenbrown.com/andersen.html

This is truly a unique find, tucked away in Victoria's most exclusive residential neighborhood: a lofty, manor house dating from 1885, superbly restored. While honoring the home's 19th-century heritage, Sylvia and Ross Main have created five contemporary suites, immense and totally private. Tall arrangements of fresh flowers in oversized vases manage to get lost in these expansive spaces. Enter the main house into a large common room, with 14-foot bay windows, a fireplace, comfortable sitting chairs, and a dining table. The Olympic Grand Suite upstairs is typical of the accommodations here. Enter a large, loft-like room through an arched doorway. The beams in the high ceiling are painted white, a barely-robin's-egg-blue between them to match the walls. Look across the room and marvel at the water and mountain views through towering 11-foot windows. Here, there's space aplenty for a king bed, fireplace, sitting chairs, and dining table. The Fairholme Grand Suite—all 850 square feet of it—has 14-foot ceilings, a double Jacuzzi tub with an ocean view, a double shower, and a mix of traditional and contemporary decor: Persian carpets on hardwood floors, oversized chairs covered in creamy-beige slip covers, a 100-year-old chandelier, and a teak dining-room table and chairs. *Directions:* From downtown, drive east on Fort St., turn right on St. Charles, right on Rockland Ave., then immediately left into Rockland Place.

FAIRHOLME MANOR
Innkeepers: Sylvia & Ross Main
638 Rockland Place
Victoria, British Columbia V8S 3R2, Canada
Tel: (250) 598-3240, Fax: (250) 598-5299
Toll Free: (877) 511-3322
6 Rooms, Double: $155–$325
Open: all year, Credit cards: all major
www.karenbrown.com/fairholmemanor.html

A wonderfully elegant manor house, Prior House features rooms of all types tucked into corners. Appearing somewhat out of nowhere, and certainly not for the faint of heart, is the Lieutenant Governor's Suite, where the bathroom is the size of a ballroom and boasts crystal chandeliers, gold swan fixtures, and a large whirlpool tub surrounded by mirrors. The Windsor Suite occupies the entire top floor with fabulous views, a private sitting room with fireplace, and air jet massage tub in the bathroom. Arbutus has a beautiful antique, queen canopied-bed covered in a rich plaid of rose, sage, and gold. It has a fireplace, a pleasant sitting area, a wonderful view of the Strait of Juan de Fuca, and a small bathroom with shower converted from a former closet. Two garden rooms with private entrances are enchanting. There's The Hobbit Room for a cozy getaway, featuring a queen bed, gas fireplace, whirlpool tub, and shower. Alternatively, The Norfolk is a spacious two room suite with large sitting area, wood-burning fireplace, and wet bar/dining area. Inside the main house, all common rooms are splendid with their heavy oak paneling and grand antiques. A beautiful, Italian chandelier graces the dining room, where six tables are handsomely set for breakfast. The library is dark and dramatic with a fireplace to lend its comforting glow. *Directions:* From downtown Blanshard St., drive east on Fort St., then south on St. Charles.

PRIOR HOUSE
Owner: Candis Cooperrider
Innkeeper: Mary Tilby
620 St. Charles
Victoria, British Columbia V8S 3N7, Canada
Tel: (250) 592-8847, Fax: (250) 592-8223
Toll Free: (877) 924-3300
6 Rooms, Double: $225–$295
Open: all year, Credit cards: MC, VS
www.karenbrown.com/prior.html

118

Places to Stay
Oregon

It's a little bit of Switzerland, a little bit of Mexico, a little bit of Morocco, and a little bit of France. It has been called a shingled sandcastle, a French-style storybook château. An environment has been created as different as possible from how, and where, one normally lives. Antiques and reproductions are intermixed in a graceful and artistic style. Intriguing architectural surprises and exquisite decorating details catch the eye at every turn. The grounds lead one to feel the tranquility of remoteness, yet the location is only ten minutes to either Cannon Beach or Manzanita. The inn has recently been acquired by Barbara Dau, who is faithfully maintaining the interior design and the lush and whimsical flowering garden as the previous owners (the Bernards) had created them. Since the inn was built as a bed & breakfast, the guestrooms are private, spacious, and well appointed. All have tiled bathrooms with stall showers, gas fireplaces, refrigerators, and concealed (sometimes ingeniously) TV/VCRs. Most rooms have views of the ocean, which lies just 250 yards from the inn across the road. An artful, hearty breakfast is served in a solarium-turreted dining room; to which is added Barbara's warmth and hospitality, and her tasteful and continually inventive cuisine. *Directions:* From the junction of Hwy 26 from Portland and Hwy 101, drive 10 miles south along the coast. The inn is on your left (look for signage).

THE ARCH CAPE HOUSE, A BED & BREAKFAST
Innkeeper: Barbara Dau
31970 East Ocean Lane
Arch Cape, OR 97102, USA
Tel: (503) 436-2800, Fax: (503) 436-1206
Toll Free: (800) 436-2848
7 Rooms, Double: $159–$239
8% room tax
Open: all year, Credit cards: all major
www.karenbrown.com/archcapehouse.html

Nestled against a hillside at the end of a quiet residential street, Country Willows embodies the perfect meeting of elegant country charm and privacy. This masterfully restored 1890s farmhouse is set on a lush, five acres of farmland only seven minutes from town. Inside the main house, enjoy a book by the fire in a library paneled in redwood, or relax in a spacious living room with a view of the Cascades. Upstairs, luxuriate in any of four handsomely appointed rooms, each decorated under the artful direction of the innkeepers. Bathrooms are immaculate and no expense is spared on details, including floors and showers made of Italian Carrara marble. All rooms have telephones, wireless internet, and magnificent views. For maximum privacy, ask about The Cottage or the stylishly converted barn housing three luxury suites with gas fireplaces and Jacuzzis and a "bunk room"—all with private decks or patios. The work of local craftsmen in these grand rooms will inspire ideas for your own dream home! Take a dip in the heated swimming pool or soak, after a day of skiing or hiking, in the outdoor hot tub. You will want for nothing in this, the ultimate country inn. *Directions:* From the south, take I-5 to Exit 11/Siskiyou Blvd, turning left on Clay in about 2 miles.

COUNTRY WILLOWS BED & BREAKFAST INN
Innkeepers: Chuck & Debbie Young
1313 Clay Street
Ashland, OR 97520, USA
Tel: (541) 488-1590, Fax: (541) 488-1611
Toll Free: (800) 945-5697
9 Rooms, Double: $125–$245
Open: all year, Credit cards: all major
www.karenbrown.com/countrywillows.html

After a varied professional career, talented innkeeper Alicia Hwang now turns her attention and superb sense of style to one of Ashland's finest inns. Morical House is at once a stunningly restored Eastlake Victorian farmhouse and a 2-acre garden; so unique, it has earned the title of Registered Backyard Habitat by the National Wildlife Federation. While respecting the building's 1882 heritage, Alicia ventures bold metropolitan touches that create an overall effect of quiet sophistication. In the entryway and main parlor, for example, East meets West in subtly stylish ways: stained-glass windows, original red-fir floors with luxurious throws, finely crafted Asian furniture, and graceful touches of color provided by the occasional orchid in a setting otherwise dominant in ivory tones and mahogany. A three-course, gourmet breakfast made with homegrown, organic ingredients is served in a simple, open, airy setting. There are nine inviting and uniquely decorated guestrooms, six in the main house and three more in the converted carriage house next door. While all are special, featuring fine linens, down pillows, and other quality appointments, the latter offer private entrances, vaulted wood ceilings, gas fireplaces, wet bars, and palatial bathrooms. The grounds are known far and wide for their exceptional beauty. *Directions:* One mile from the town center heading north on Main out of town.

MORICAL HOUSE GARDEN INN
Innkeeper: Alicia Y. Hwang
668 North Main Street
Ashland, OR 97520, USA
Tel: (541) 482-2254, Fax: (541) 482-1775
Toll Free: (800) 208-0960
9 Rooms, Double: $130–$250
Open: all year, Credit cards: all major
www.karenbrown.com/morical.html

Long, narrow hallways of wood and brick, high ceilings, curved staircases, and reproduction gaslight fixtures make it easy to imagine what the Peerless Hotel must have looked, and felt like, during its heyday at the beginning of the 20th century when Ashland was a key stop on the Southern Pacific Railroad's Siskiyou Line. A red-brick building, once a popular boarding house for railroad employees, the Peerless retains the flavor of its early Victorian charm, even as it offers every amenity the 21st-century traveler expects in a quality hotel. Now on the National Register of Historic Places, due to the heroic restoration achievements of owner Crissy Barnett, this inn is great fun. Crissy adds an eclectic touch to each of the four rooms and two suites, whether it's a floor-to-ceiling mural painted by a local artist or "his and hers" claw-foot bathtubs. Bathrooms are uncommonly spacious, many with Jacuzzi tub-shower combinations or two-person showers. Bed linens hail from Italy and luxurious floral fabrics and wallpaper patterns unite creatively with the wood-and-brick interiors. Breakfast is served across the courtyard-garden in the Peerless Restaurant. Start your day at a graciously decorated table next to the fireplace. The restaurant is also open for dinner, an outstanding, contemporary, Pacific Northwest dining experience in a casually elegant setting. *Directions:* In the Historic Railroad District on 4th between A and B Streets.

❄ ☕ ▭ ☎ Y P ⑪ 🖊 ♿ 🚶 🏇 ⛷ 🍷

PEERLESS HOTEL
Innkeeper: Crissy Barnett
243 Fourth Street
Ashland, OR 97520, USA
Tel: (541) 488-1082, Fax: (541) 488-5508
Toll Free: (800) 460-8758
6 Rooms, Double: $74–$242
Dinner: Tue-Sun
Closed: Jan, Credit cards: all major
Select Registry
www.karenbrown.com/peerless.html

Named for its original owners, not for Shakespeare's character, the Romeo Inn is a large and gracious retreat, built in the Cape Cod style in the 1930s and set on a half-acre of land in a quiet residential neighborhood. All four guestrooms and two luxurious suites offer king-sized beds, private baths, telephones, data ports, and wireless internet. Grab a plushy towel and head out to the heated swimming pool or hot tub. Lie in the hammock in a quiet corner of the terraced garden. Sneak out to the kitchen for a cookie or enjoy the handsome library nook well-stocked with good reading. Deana and Don Politis anticipate guests' every desire in this thoroughly graceful, contemporary, and spacious setting. Upstairs, the exquisitely English-country Bristol and Coventry rooms are cheerful and spotless, each offering a writing desk, window seat, and built-in bookshelves. Downstairs, the Canterbury and Windsor rooms are especially grand with richly colored walls and lovely fabrics. The former boasts a floor-to-ceiling brick fireplace. The Cambridge Suite provides overstuffed chairs in front of a tiled fireplace and French doors onto a private patio. Detached from the inn and completely self-sufficient, the Stratford Suite sits high above the street, with views of the Cascades, the valley, and the inn's garden. *Directions:* Just before Main Street becomes Siskiyou Blvd heading south, turn right on Gresham, left on Iowa, then right on Idaho.

ROMEO INN
Innkeepers: Deana & Don Politis
295 Idaho Street
Ashland, OR 97520, USA
Tel: (541) 488-0884, Toll Free: (800) 915-8899
6 Rooms, Double: $140–$200
Open: all year, Credit cards: MC, VS
www.karenbrown.com/romeo.html

For a delightfully offbeat experience, consider renting the single cottage on the Weisinger Vineyard property just 4 miles south of town. Originally a storage space for apples, this 576-square-foot structure has been cleverly converted to create a snug and private retreat surrounded by acres of vineyard. With a panoramic view from the deck of the Rogue Valley, the vineyard, and the Cascade and Siskiyou Mountains, you'll love the simple, rustic charm of this space, complete with a gas fireplace and a private outdoor hot tub. In the bedroom, rest your head in a queen-sized, four-poster bed. The living area is cozily arranged with a fully equipped kitchen, a clean bathroom with large shower, a TV, VCR, books, binoculars, and a CD/cassette player. The Weisingers prepare a lovely welcome basket of complimentary wine, cheese, crackers, and other goodies. Stroll up to the Tasting Room to meet the family, whose warm and genuine hospitality will make you feel very much at home. Premium, handcrafted wines from local fruit have won the Weisingers numerous national and international awards. In summertime, assemble a picnic basket from the deli selections in the Tasting Room. Traffic on I-5 does account for some noise; but privacy, setting, and welcome more than make up for it. *Directions:* Take Siskiyou Blvd south out of town. Four miles from the Shakespeare Festival grounds, turn right into the Weisinger Winery and follow the signs from the driveway.

WEISINGER'S VINEYARD COTTAGE
Innkeeper: John Weisinger
3150 Siskiyou Boulevard
Ashland, OR 97520, USA
Tel & Fax: (541) 488-5989
Toll Free: (800) 551-WINE
1 cottage: $175*
*Breakfast not included
Open: all year, Credit cards: MC, VS
www.karenbrown.com/weisingers.html

Ashland contains many historic buildings, among them the Winchester Inn, Restaurant & Wine Bar built in 1886 as a private home, and at one time used as a hospital. Its quiet but central location, two blocks south of the Shakespeare Festival grounds and one block above Main Street, makes it perfect for coming home to relax between shopping excursions or attending one of the many theatrical performances. Guestrooms are found in two historic Victorian and two additional buildings, all cleverly woven together with walkways and gardens. Bedrooms all have a Victorian flair and come in a large variety of shapes and sizes—some can accommodate an extra bed and there are several suites and apartments suitable for families. Bathrooms in the more deluxe guestrooms have both showers and Jacuzzi or whirlpool tubs. We loved our luxurious accommodation in the Robert Gordon Suite with its spacious sitting room, king bed, and whirlpool tub. Breakfast—fruit, juice, freshly baked pastries, and a choice of three cooked entrees—is served on the spacious garden patio in summer, in the dining room in winter. Be sure to include dinner at the inn in your Ashland dining plans. *Directions:* From I-5 north, take Exit 11 and follow Siskiyou Boulevard into town till it becomes a one-way street. Turn left on Second Street, cross Main Street, and the inn is on your right.

WINCHESTER INN, RESTAURANT & WINE BAR
Innkeepers: Michael & Laurie Gibbs
35 South Second Street
Ashland, OR 97520, USA
Tel: (541) 488-1115, Fax: (541) 488-4604
Toll Free: (800) 972-4991
19 Rooms, Double: $175–$250
Open: all year, Credit cards: all major
www.karenbrown.com/winchesterinn.html

Talk about pampering! Jim and Tracy have thought of everything. There are cookies and milk at bedtime and breakfast options as extensive as your imagination, from chocolate-chip bread pudding with orange rum sauce to eggs Benedict to cinnamon rolls. Comfortable, completely low key, a tad kitsch, and genuinely fun, Cricketwood is a perfect place to stay when exploring the Bend area. There's a hot tub on the deck, wine and beer in the fridge all day, a 2-mile loop for walking or running on the 10-acre property, stellar mountain views, wild ducks, videos, popcorn, peanuts. Guestrooms are a scream. Check out the full-scale urinal in the Secret Garden's bathroom. Or Enchanted Forest where in three unique alcoves you'll find a king and two double beds. At the entry to each alcove is a swath of sheer nylon in an iridescent green, reminiscent of mosquito netting. It has a large table, recliner-couch, and a spacious bathroom with jungle mural, a shower, and a two-person hydrotherapy tub. A cottage with a two-person spa tub, see-though fireplace, and full kitchen (plus pets are accepted) is available. *Directions:* From Bend, take Hwy 97 north and turn right on Greenwood (Hwy 20/Burns). Turn left at the flashing yellow light, half a mile past Barnes and Noble (Hamby). Go 3 miles, turn right on Repine (gravel road), and then left on Cricketwood.

❄ 🛋 🚵 💳 ☎ 🐕 ♈ P 🚭 🌼 🏃 🥾 🐎 ⛷ 🚣 🍇

CRICKETWOOD COUNTRY BED & BREAKFAST
Innkeepers: Jim & Tracy Duncan
63520 Cricketwood Road
Bend, OR 97701, USA
Tel: (541) 330-0747, Fax: (541) 312-9389
Toll Free: (877) 330-0747
3 Rooms, Double: $95–$135
1 cottage
Open: all year, Credit cards: all major
www.karenbrown.com/cricketwood.html

Stephanie has presence. She's a large, two-level, cedar-shingled building with several huge stone chimneys, and sits right on the beach. Step through beveled-glass front doors into a gracious lobby dominated by thick pillars of unfinished wood and exposed hardware. The gas fireplace is lit, the classical music calms, and the lighting is low and warm. Behind the entryway, you find a wonderfully inviting sitting room with huge bay windows overlooking the Pacific Ocean, comfortable couches in leather or rich fabrics, hardwood floors, a piano, and a fireplace. Guestrooms are handsomely decorated with open wood beams, quality wood furniture, and Northwest fabrics in attractive deep, rich tones. Wainscoting and white walls characterize the modern bathrooms; toilets reside behind their own doors. Most rooms have a Jacuzzi tub for two, gas fireplace, TV/DVD players, and a deck; but even the smallest rooms are charming. One-bedroom suites decorated in a French country style are available in the neighboring Carriage House. There are two TVs in these suites and beautiful light fixtures in the bathrooms. A full breakfast is served in an intimate upstairs dining room overlooking the Coastal Mountains. Dinner is available seven days a week. *Directions:* From the north, take Hwy 101 to the third Cannon Beach exit. Turn right at the fork to Hemlock then right on Matanuska.

❄ 🍵 ▣ ☎ 🛗 Y P ⑪ 🚭 ⛷ ☂ 🚶 👫 🏇 🍇

STEPHANIE INN
Manager: Sharon Major
2740 S. Pacific
P. O. Box 219
Cannon Beach, OR 97110, USA
Tel: (503) 436-2221, Fax: (503) 436-9711
Toll Free: (800) 633-3466
50 Rooms, Double: $229–$489
Open: all year, Credit cards: all major
www.karenbrown.com/stephanie.html

When's the last time you enjoyed cabaña service on the beach? From Memorial Day to Labor Day, you can expect it at Surfsand Resort, where hale and hardy lads set up lawn chairs and windbreaks. When we visited, the resort was hard at work preparing for summer activity: building a new beachside deck and preparing for a new set of rooms which now include high-speed wireless internet access. This is a great choice for families who are looking for quality accommodations; a pampering, friendly, energetic staff; and lots of events for the kids: sandcastle competitions, kite-flying, and even a dog show. Several different styles of rooms are available, so ask the reservationist to help you select the right one. Whether you choose a studio or a spacious suite, all rooms are well appointed. The oceanfront Jacuzzi suites are the best in terms of space and decor: very handsome and contemporary. All have at least partial views of the beach, Haystack Rock, Ecola State Park, and Tillamook Head Lighthouse. An indoor swimming pool and whirlpool are available. Ask about private home rentals as well. *Directions:* From the north, take Hwy 101 to the first Cannon Beach exit. Turn right at the fork to Hemlock then right on Gower.

SURFSAND RESORT
Manager: Chad Sweet
Oceanfront at Gower
Cannon Beach, OR 97110, USA
Tel: (503) 436-2274, Fax: (503) 436-9116
Toll Free: (800) 547-6100
83 Rooms, Double: $199–$359*
8 cottages
*Breakfast not included: $5–$16
Open: all year, Credit cards: all major
www.karenbrown.com/surfsand.html

Take this particular spot on the Oregon coast, marry it to the stellar service and hospitality that the innkeepers provide, and you've got more than you need. At Channel House, you'd be willing to sleep on a futon and would still come away calling it one of the best places to stay. Many coastal inns lay claim to ocean views—many are prettier—but nothing equals this unique spot for sheer wildness. Created here is the sense that you are as directly in contact with the ocean, as you might be in a lighthouse on an island in the middle of it. This is especially so from your outdoor Jacuzzi tub, poised almost precariously on your own private deck. You just can't get closer to the Pacific without boarding a ship. The gray-shingled building doesn't look like anything from the outside; but all the bedrooms, whether a single room or a corner suite, feel hugely dramatic, exposed, invigorating and are newly decorated. Buy a bottle of wine in the lobby downstairs, then light the fire and jump into that balcony tub. Not just an ocean view— it's an adventure. Channel House is one of our favorites, even compared to much more luxurious alternatives. It's genuine, natural, unaffected, romantic, and very private. *Directions:* From the north on Hwy 101, enter Depoe Bay, proceed through the traffic signal, cross the bridge, and take your first right. The inn is on the right.

CHANNEL HOUSE
Owners: Vicki & Carl Finseth
Manager: Bart Barrowclough
35 Ellingson Street
Depoe Bay, OR 97341, USA
Tel: (541) 765-2140, Fax: (541) 765-2191
Toll Free: (800) 447-2140
12 Rooms, Double: $225–$320
Open: all year, Credit cards: all major
Select Registry
www.karenbrown.com/channel.html

In this delightful boutique hotel, each of the guestrooms are so truly different in look and feel, it's best to let Myra Plant and her attentive staff recommend the right one for you. While every modern convenience imaginable awaits you in this shingled, Queen Anne/Craftsman home, the presentation is old-world European all the way. As in European hotels, space can sometimes be a bit cramped in places; but the overall effect is one of such character and charm, you shouldn't miss the experience. Some rooms are simple and soothing with dormer windows, gabled ceilings, and claw-foot tubs; while others are bright and cheerful, or stately and tailored with paisley wallpaper even in the bathroom. Still others are wildly dramatic, with music piped in and gas fireplaces. You must see the sumptuous Rachel, for example, where great, rich bursts of floral patterns are boldly and fantastically coordinated—a sort of Laura Ashley meets William Randolph Hearst that works completely! Tea, coffee, and cookies are available. The Dining Room serves 2–5 course dinners, including wine, Wednesday to Saturday. Campbell House leaves a lasting impression long after you've pulled away, not only for the marvelously unusual rooms and lovely grounds, but for the professional and genuine service. *Directions:* Leave I-5 north at Exit 194B, taking I-105 west. Leave at Exit 2 and turn left at the "Y." Cross the river and take the Downtown Exit. Turn right onto Pearl.

CAMPBELL HOUSE
Innkeeper: Myra Plant
252 Pearl Street
Eugene, OR 97401, USA
Tel: (541) 343-1119, Fax: (541) 343-2258
Toll Free: (800) 264-2519
18 Rooms, Double: $119–$345
1 cottage: $245–$345
Open: all year, Credit cards: all major
Select Registry
www.karenbrown.com/campbell.html

Conveniently located on a tree-lined residential street in Eugene's downtown area and only blocks from the university, the Oval Door is a lovely, contemporary, three-story farmhouse-style home, originally built to serve as an inn. Your innkeepers are chefs so you know that breakfast and other culinary treats are going to be special. These talented women have created a simple yet elegant setting, where you can have as much or as little privacy as you need, but always lots of pampering. All five guestrooms, fresh and generously appointed, are named after Oregon wildflowers and are practical and luxurious in artfully understated ways. Queen Anne's Lace presents a 19th-century design with a mahogany queen bed, sitting area with sofa, and access to a separate Jacuzzi tub room with heated towel bars. Wild Rose offers a softly romantic setting with a queen iron bed and a single daybed. Forget-Me-Not is a sweet, charming room with an up-stepping queen brass bed. For ultimate privacy, the self-sufficient Morning Glory "honeymoon suite" is hidden away on the third floor with a custom-made, king-sized, iron bed handcrafted to resemble vines and morning glory buds, a 6-foot soaking tub, and every reason not to venture far. *Directions:* From I-5, exit 194B west to the end of the freeway (Jefferson). Continue on after the light for three blocks. Turn left on 10th, continue for almost two blocks, then turn left into the driveway behind the inn.

OVAL DOOR BED & BREAKFAST INN
Innkeepers: Nicole Craig & Melissa McGuire
988 Lawrence Street
Eugene, OR 97401, USA
Tel: (541) 683-3160, Fax: (541) 485-0260
Toll Free: (800) 882-3160
5 Rooms, Double: $85–$195
Open: all year, Credit cards: all major
www.karenbrown.com/oval.html

Tu Tu' Tun is a delightful, small fishing lodge hugging the banks of the Rogue River, 7 miles from the coast. Although it is appealing at first glance, when you go inside you realize how truly special Tu Tu' Tun Lodge is and why its rooms are booked solid all season. The heart of the inn includes a spacious lounge with a massive, stone fireplace and a wall of windows facing the river, an intimate bar, cozy library, and a nationally acclaimed, gourmet dining room. A separate two-story wing, joined by a walkway to the lounge-dining area, houses the guestrooms. All have tall windows overlooking the river and decks or patios with dramatic views. Many of the bedrooms have fireplaces and some even have outdoor soaking tubs. Throughout the lodge, the furnishings are of fine quality and the tasteful decor exudes a rustic, yet sophisticated, simplicity. Stretching across the entire side of the lodge, facing the intensely green water of the Rogue, is a large deck—a favorite place for guests to relax. Terraced below the deck is a swimming pool, and below that the lawn sweeps down to the banks of the river where there is a small boat pier from which guests leave each morning for fishing excursions or jet-boat trips up the Rogue. *Directions:* From Gold Beach, drive north over the bridge and immediately turn right on the North Rogue. Continue for about 6 miles, following signs for the inn.

TU TU' TUN LODGE
Innkeepers: Laurie & Dirk Van Zante
96550 North Bank Rogue
Gold Beach, OR 97444, USA
Tel: (541) 247-6664, Fax: (541) 247-0672
Toll Free: (800) 864-6357
20 Rooms, Double: $195–$500*
2 cottages
*Breakfast not included: $13, Meal Package $52.50
Open: all year, Credit cards: MC, VS
www.karenbrown.com/tututunlodge.html

Designed for one-time Oregon lumber magnate and philanthropist Simon Benson, the Columbia Gorge Hotel has been a Hood River favorite since 1921. The Italian stonemasons, brought to America to construct the Columbia River Highway, are also responsible for building the stone walls and bridges you'll see on this 11-acre property, poised high on a cliff above the magnificent Columbia River Gorge at the top of a 208-foot waterfall. Dramatic surroundings make this hotel memorable, but the warm hospitality of the staff is also remarkable. Hotel staff wear traditional uniforms in this formal setting, but greet and serve you in the casual, friendly Pacific-Northwest manner. Caviar and champagne are served in the Valentino Lounge every evening, a handsome room with piano, bar, and a small dance floor. Upstairs, just 40 guestrooms keep this hotel intimate and offer a choice of garden view, river view, and specialty rooms. If at all possible, however, get a room on the river side, throw open your screenless windows, and let fresh air and the sound of the waterfall lull you to sleep. Wake to stellar views of the gorge and national forests. The modestly appointed rooms are decorated in colors reminiscent of years past, and include telephones with data ports, television sets, and the best mattresses. A huge breakfast is served in the dining room overlooking the gorge. *Directions:* From Portland, take I-84 east to Exit 62. Turn left and follow the signs.

❄ ☕ 💳 ☎ 🐕 🛗 ⅄ P 🍴 🖼 🚶

COLUMBIA GORGE HOTEL
Manager: Karl Wells
4000 Westcliff Drive
Hood River, OR 97031, USA
Tel: (541) 386-5566, Fax: (541) 386-9141
Toll Free: (800) 345-1921
40 Rooms, Double: $199–$359
Open: all year, Credit cards: all major
Select Registry
www.karenbrown.com/columbia.html

This beautiful home, nestled on three acres of woodland and riverfront, overlooks the Columbia River. Understandably, the Pates fell in love with Lakecliff; as Allyson said, she felt she was sent here. We, too, fell in love with Lakecliff—first with the image of the home framed by trees with a dramatic backdrop of river, then, upon entry, the embrace of fresh, light, warm and inviting décor. The handsome living room with leather sofas set before a dramatic river stone fireplace looks out through a large window framing the river view. Adjacent, the dining room opens to a deck with tables shaded by a 40-year-old wisteria. On a stretch of the river, referred to as The Hatchery by locals (great for windsurfing), hundreds of sails enhance the picture in season. Four guestrooms with queen beds are available: three with fireplaces and three with river views on the second floor. Forget Me Not is a very pretty end room in soft blue and yellows. Center, Lilac, the original master suite, enjoys a fireplace and in-room sink (with its toilet and shower across the hall). Daffodil, the other end room considered the choice room, was converted from what was the master suite sitting area and has corner windows, fireplace and private bath. Overlooking the front garden, the "Garden Room" is very tranquil and has a fireplace. The Pates are committed to spoil our guests. *Directions:* From Portland, take I-84 east to exit 62. Turn left off the exit, then right on Westcliff Drive.

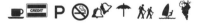

LAKECLIFF
Innkeepers: Allyson & James Pates
3820 Westcliff Drive
Hood River, OR 97031, USA
Tel: (541) 386-7000
4 Rooms, Double: $125–$150
Open: all year, Credit cards: MC, VS
www.karenbrown.com/lakecliff.html

Jacksonville was a boom town in the later part of the 19th century after gold was discovered in the area in 1851. Fortunately for today's visitors, this quaint little town "slept" for most of the 20th century, only to be rediscovered by tourism when it was recognized as a National Historic Landmark. Sitting in the heart of town, the Jacksonville Inn started off as the Ryan and Morgan General Store then had several other lives before its latest and very lovely reincarnation. As you register in the wine shop you realize that choosing a wine with dinner could be an evening-long event—the store has over 2000 selections! Upstairs, the bedrooms retain the flavor of early-Victorian charm while offering all the amenities of a quality hotel. All have shower rooms; one enjoys a steam shower and another a whirlpool tub. For total seclusion, opt for one of the four honeymoon cottages found on an adjacent quiet residential street. Latourette is an especially decadent cottage with its three-sided fireplace dividing the bedroom from the sitting room and facing the Jacuzzi tub. There's also a shower and steam room. We attest to the food being absolutely excellent, from evening-long four-course meals to simpler bistro fare. In summer the Britt Festivals take place in a beautiful amphitheater three blocks from the hotel. *Directions:* From I-5 north, take Exit 40 and go south on Old Stage Road to Jacksonville where you find the Jacksonville Inn at 175 California Street.

❄ ☕ 🍴 CREDIT ☎ 🍷 P 🍴 ≋ 🚣 ⛷ 🏃 👫 🎿 ⛷ 🍇

JACKSONVILLE INN
Innkeepers: Linda & Jerry Evans
P.O. Box 359
Jacksonville, OR 97530, USA
Tel: (541) 899-1900, Fax: (541) 899-1373
Toll Free: (800) 321-9344
8 Rooms, Double: $149–$189
4 cottages: $250–$450
Open: all year, Credit cards: all major
Select Registry
www.karenbrown.com/jacksonvilleinn.html

When you begin the 700-foot ascent along a meandering road to this inn, all you see in any direction are miles of rolling hills, vineyards, and farmhouses. Suddenly you round that last bend, spot your destination, and catch your breath. This amazing 10,000-square-foot house, set on 50 acres of land, is spectacular, as are the views from it! Youngberg Hill has one vision: crafting a small amount of exceptional Pinot Noir using only estate-grown fruit and creating a stellar setting for guests to enjoy the results. Owner Nicolette happily conducts tastings for guests. This striking multi-level house features four elegantly appointed rooms and three suites. These rooms are palatial, and all offer unparalleled views of the Willamette Valley. There are no TVs here, but all other comforts abound. Consider treating yourself to the Martini Suite: private balcony with views on two sides, separate sitting room with fireplace two-person Jacuzzi tub . . . stunning. On the first floor, have your pick of rooms for relaxing, each with access to a covered deck overlooking the panorama. *Directions:* From Portland, drive south on I-5 to Hwy 99W. After Dundee, take Route 18–McMinnville bypass. Go 10 miles to the Masonville Road, turn right and go 2 miles to Youngberg Hill Road. Turn right and after 1 mile look for a sign on the left.

YOUNGBERG HILL VINEYARDS & INN
Innkeeper: Nicolette Bailey
10660 Youngberg Hill Road
McMinnville, OR 97128, USA
Tel: (503) 472-2727, Fax: (503) 472-1313
Toll Free: (888) 657-8668
7 Rooms, Double: $149–$269
Open: all year, Credit cards: MC, VS
www.karenbrown.com/youngberg.html

Every choice made during the creation of the Pine Meadow Inn was motivated by a desire to slow the pace, to soothe the weary soul. Situated on 9 acres of Douglas fir and Ponderosa pine, this utterly delightful retreat was designed to resemble the farmhouse-style homes that Maloy remembers from his boyhood in the Midwest. From the large wraparound porch, you can watch the deer and jackrabbits that love this spot. Once inside, you'll find a cozy sitting room and fireplace, beautifully crafted by master carpenters. French doors open from the dining room onto an exquisite English cutting garden, where paths lead to the hot tub on a redwood deck under the pines, or down to the koi pond. Upstairs, four large and restful guestrooms are appointed with turn-of-the-century antiques and queen-sized beds. The telephone is hidden in the closet so that you don't have to look at it if you don't want to. Count, instead, on fresh flowers, extra pillows, and cookies on your nightstand before bedtime. Nancy and Maloy's genuine warmth of welcome and love of their surroundings is catching—you'll definitely want to return. Merlin, just minutes from Grants Pass, is considered the center of activity for the wildest and most scenic sections of the Rogue River. *Directions:* Take I-5 north to Exit 61/Merlin, turning left off the ramp. Drive 5 miles through Merlin, cross a small bridge, and go right on Crow Road for 1 mile. Follow signs at the end of Crow.

PINE MEADOW INN
Innkeepers: Nancy & Maloy Murdock
1000 Crow Road
Merlin (Grants Pass), OR 97532, USA
Tel & Fax: (541) 471-6277
Toll Free: (800) 554-0806
4 Rooms, Double: $95–$130
Closed: Nov to Jan, Credit cards: all major
www.karenbrown.com/pinemeadow.html

Paul Romans grew up on the very spot the Mount Hood Hamlet Bed & Breakfast occupies. In those days however he was a boy milking cows! Eighteenth-century New England Colonial elegance in a pastoral setting describes this delightful new home in the beautiful Hood River Valley, with its unsurpassed views of Mount Hood. Furnishings often complement the period architecture, but there are contemporary touches as well. A "see-through" wood-burning fireplace separates the cozy library from a large living room with lots of windows and good books. Original art and old maps adorn the walls, including many watercolors of English landscapes. Oriental carpets cover floors. Adjoining the dining room is an inviting "garden room" that opens to an outdoor deck with hot tub. The floors in this room, and in the area immediately surrounding the tub are heated, making wintertime transitions to and fro a gentler experience. Bedrooms are wonderful—even the smallest is spacious and well-appointed, with excellent lighting, plush robes, and walk-in closets. Bathrooms are spotless and modern. All rooms have TVs, VCRs, fireplaces and ready access to a selection of movies. From the Jacuzzi tub in the Vista Ridge room, you can see Mount Hood if you keep the bathroom door open. *Directions:* From Hood River, take Hwy 35 south to the town of Mount Hood. Pass the general store at the Parkdale junction. Turn left into the inn's drive after 2/10 mile.

MOUNT HOOD HAMLET BED & BREAKFAST
Innkeepers: Diane & Paul Romans
6741 Hwy 35
Mount Hood, OR 97041, USA
Tel: (541) 352-3574, Fax: (541) 352-7685
Toll Free: (800) 407-0570
4 Rooms, Double: $125–$150
Open: all year, Credit cards: all major
www.karenbrown.com/mthood.html

Situated on 70 acres, this enchanting hazelnut farm property with four matching Craftsman-style buildings is pure magic. Only 20 minutes from Portland, you'll swear that you are in the Italian countryside. The entry hall in the Main House is extraordinary, painted and papered in buoyantly bold yellows and blues, with a ceiling right out of, say, old Mexico. Notice the piano, the fireplace, the glassed-in sun porch, the orchids—and you haven't even left the entryway! This is a welcoming, whimsical house with grand public rooms. Situated on the grounds, separate from the main house, are the Carriage House and Rose Cottage. In the Carriage House, ascend a wooden staircase and enter old-country, just perfect for a long stay with a master bedroom, claw-foot bathtub, big living room, and a perfectly equipped kitchen. Or try the Rose Cottage, restored to its original state with fir floors, high ceilings, tiled fireplace, a little kitchen, and laundry facilities. Settle in as there is lots to do. Take the canoe out on the pond, surrounded in spring by thousands of daffodils. Go for a swim in the pool. Enjoy a game of tennis. Sample wine in the renovated barn. *Directions:* From Portland, take I-5 south to the Tigard exit, then take 99W for about 14 miles to milepost 21. The farm is on the right.

SPRINGBROOK HAZELNUT FARM
Innkeepers: Ellen & Chuck McClure
30295 North Hwy 99W
Newberg, OR 97132, USA
Tel: (503) 538-4606
Toll Free: (800) 793-8528
2 Cottages: $225
Open: all year, Credit cards: MC, VS
www.karenbrown.com/springbrook.html

Originally The Bradshaw Boarding House (in 1900) and later a bordello, the charmingly mysterious Oar House is a marvel of Jan Johnson's imagination. She has taken impossible spaces and idiosyncrasies of construction and crafted a unique and sophisticated inn decorated with Persian carpets, Oriental objects d'art, nautical paraphernalia, and other eclectic assortments. The Crow's Nest is perhaps the most delightful space, best suited to someone under 6 feet tall. It's a third-floor attic space that Jan has ingeniously recrafted into a fanciful, yet urbane, guestroom with queen bed and sitting area taking advantage of the ocean view. It has a beautiful, modern bathroom with huge soaking tub and neighbors a ship's ladder that leads to an enclosed cupola, complete with widow's walk, offering 360-degree views of the area. The Starboard has a whirlpool tub for two and views of the ocean and Yaquina Head Lighthouse. Nowhere in America have we seen such a steep and irregular staircase and so many unusual nooks and crannies. Jan is also an exceptional cook, so breakfast in the ocean view dining area will be special. The central sitting areas reminded us of a 16th-century English cottage with low, beamed ceilings and shuttered windows. *Directions:* At the intersection of Hwy 101 and Hurbert Street (one stoplight south of Hwy 20) go west on Hurbert for three blocks to SW Second and turn left.

OAR HOUSE BED & BREAKFAST
Innkeepers: Jan & Keith Johnson
520 SW Second Street
Newport, OR 97365, USA
Tel: (541) 265-9571, Fax: none
Toll Free: (800) 252-2358
4 Rooms, Double: $140–$150
Open: all year, Credit cards: MC, VS
www.karenbrown.com/oarhouse.html

Maybe it's the well-insulated walls, but Tyee Lodge feels especially quiet from any corner of any room. Set in a tranquil neighborhood on the shores of Agate Beach, this low-key, friendly, but sophisticated inn offers five very inviting guestrooms. Each is decorated in similar Northwest tones of green and burgundy, and includes a handsome selection of Early American Indian and local art. Guestrooms have names like Chinook, Siletz, Tillamook, and Alsea. All have low-sitting queen beds with down comforters, gas fireplaces (some of the woodstove variety), at least 40 square feet of glass and windows, and good modern bathrooms graced with skylights. Walk down a private trail lined with scenic shore pines to the beach and tide pools. Enjoy a book by the fire or the complimentary wine service in the windowed common room. Located north of Newport's town center, Tyee Lodge is just minutes away from Hatfield Marine Science Center, the Oregon Coast Aquarium, Nye Beach historic oceanfront village, and other coastal attractions. Yaquina Head, where you can tour the lighthouse, is only a short drive or walk away. A gourmet breakfast is served in the dining room downstairs. *Directions:* Approximately 3 miles north of the main intersection of Hwy 20 and US 101. Woody Way and Lucky Gap Trail fork off a public parking access point along US 101 just south of Lighthouse Drive.

TYEE LODGE
Innkeepers: Monty & Brenda Roberts
4925 NW Woody Way
Newport, OR 97365, USA
Tel: (541) 265-8953, Fax: none
Toll Free: (888) 553-8933
5 Rooms, Double: $120–$160
Open: all year, Credit cards: all major
www.karenbrown.com/tyee.html

Early in the 20th century, Simon Benson—lumber baron, philanthropist, visionary—
decided that Portland needed its own grand accommodations for visitors. Completed in
1912, his namesake hotel was—and still is—luxurious; the oldest continuously operating
hotel in the city. Graced by Austrian crystal chandeliers, Circassian walnut walls, and
Italian marble floors, the palatial lobby exudes an air of quiet sophistication. This is
Portland's only five-star hotel. It's where the President stays when he comes to town. In
fact, every president since Harry Truman has done so. Rooms are accessed from softly lit
hallways that may remind you of those on luxury cruise liners of old, complete with
beautiful hardwood doors. All guestrooms, as you might expect, provide modern luxury
in a classic setting. Whether you choose something specially appointed or an elegant
standard room, you can count on a state-of-the-art entertainment system, an honor bar,
round-the-clock room service, and generally high style. Set the mood for a romantic
evening with dinner at The London Grill, the epitome of luxury in rich, dark tones, with
classical music and candlelit tables dressed with white linen and orchids. *Directions:*
From the airport, take I-84 west to I-5 south, following signs to City Center. Cross
Morrison Bridge, turn right on 2nd Street, go two blocks to Oak, and turn left. The
Benson is at Oak and Broadway.

THE BENSON
Manager: Ron Gladney
309 SW Broadway
Portland, OR 97205, USA
Tel: (503) 228-2000, Fax: (503) 226-4603
287 Rooms, Double: $199–$900*
*Breakfast not included: $12
Open: all year, Credit cards: all major
www.karenbrown.com/benson.html

Upon entering the lobby of this handsome historic hotel, guests are greeted by a massive mural that takes them back to the early history of the Northwest. Mural artist Melinda Morey traces the journey of explorers Lewis and Clark, who blazed a trail from Missouri to the Pacific Ocean in 1804-06. Here are Native Americans fishing for salmon at Celilo Falls on the Columbia River, Lewis trading with the Nez Perce, Sacajawea marveling at the blue Pacific. A Northwest theme prevails throughout The Governor in warm tones of sage, rust, gold, and brown. Handcrafted marquetry, terracotta ornamentation, mahogany detailing, leather club chairs around a crackling fire, a totem pole, tables made from cross sections of felled trees—all add up to an atmosphere of drama and richness. Notice the wall sconces in the hallways outside each bedroom and wonderful reproduction prints from the Lewis and Clark journal or black-and-white photographs of local Indian tribes of long ago. While the setting is historic, service is unquestionably contemporary. Rooms are cleverly designed in keeping with the hotel's theme, and amenities include everything you would expect in a full-service hotel. Some have fireplaces, wet bars, jet baths, terraces, or skylights—you need only ask. Jake's Grill with its carved wood columns and mounted wild game is right downstairs. *Directions:* Beaverton/City Center. Exit at Salmon Street and go right on 10th to the corner of Alder.

THE GOVERNOR HOTEL
Manager: Jeff Fleming
Director: Sara Herschberger
611 SW 11th Avenue
Portland, OR 97205, USA
Tel: (503) 224-3400, Fax: (503) 241-2122
Toll Free: (800) 554-3456
100 Rooms, Double: $189–$259*
*Breakfast not included
Open: all year, Credit cards: all major
www.karenbrown.com/governorhotel.html

Positioned as it is in the heart of Portland's cultural district, adjacent to the symphony, the art museum, and the Center for Performing Arts; The Heathman chooses to make the most of its artistic associations with many unique surprises, not the least of which are copies of Andy Warhol's ten-part Endangered Species silkscreen collection. There's a lending library on the mezzanine level from which guests borrow books signed by authors who have stayed at the hotel (to date there are more than 1,000 in the collection). Also on this level, artwork loaned by the local Elizabeth Leach Gallery is rotated every seven weeks. Bedrooms are tailored to include a king-sized bed, a fully-stocked bar, a French coffee press, an armoire with television and drawers, a desk, and two multi-line telephones with complimentary high-speed internet access. Bathrooms have shower/tub combinations with plenty of upgraded soaps and shampoos. At no additional charge, a 500-title video movie library is available to guests. In the Grand Room, afternoon tea is served seasonally, then the room is transformed for cocktails and live jazz five nights a week. Eucalyptus wood paneling in the Grand Room is original, as is the beautiful rosewood in the elevator. The Heathman is not without a sense of humor—ask to see the Andy Warhol Suite! *Directions:* Beaverton/City Center. Exit at Salmon Street then drive eight blocks to Broadway.

THE HEATHMAN
Manager: Jeff Jobe
1001 SW Broadway
Portland, OR 97205, USA
Tel: (503) 241-4100, Fax: (503) 790-7110
Toll Free: (800) 551-0011
150 Rooms, Double: $169–$750*
*Breakfast not included
Open: all year, Credit cards: all major
www.karenbrown.com/heathman.html

In spite of the grandeur of this 10,000-square-foot English Tudor home, there is nothing the least bit pretentious about Heron Haus. Rather, the delightful Julie Keppeler has created a low-key, informal environment that makes guests feel every bit as much at home as she does. This unbelievably spacious urban home, commanding panoramic views of the city from the top of Nob Hill, spreads over three rambling levels in a sort of tree-house pattern. Our guest room, Kulia, was immense with a queen-sized bed, a roomy sitting area, and a long built-in desk overlooking the city. The bathroom was nearly as big as the bedroom, with a two-person Jacuzzi tub surrounded on two sides by windows, a wicker chair, and a gas fireplace. Julie has performed wonders with the third-floor attic space to create thoroughly magical sleeping and sitting areas. Furnishings are simple and unassuming throughout. Colors are bright and cheerful. Endless windows are covered in handsome plantation shutters. A simple and satisfying breakfast is ready at your convenience in the large dining area in front of a fire. It's an easy walk to Portland's finest eateries and boutique shops in "The Village" on 23rd Street. *Directions:* From downtown, take Glison to the Nob Hill district. Turn right on NW 24th Avenue then left on NW Johnson, which becomes Westover. Just before Westover makes a sharp U-turn and goes up the hill, pull straight into the narrow driveway marked 2545.

HERON HAUS
Innkeeper: Julie Beacon Keppeler
2545 NW Westover Road
Portland, OR 97210, USA
Tel: (503) 274-1846, Fax: (503) 248-4055
6 Rooms, Double: $135–$350*
*Breakfast not included: $6.5
Open: all year, Credit cards: MC, VS
Select Registry
www.karenbrown.com/heron.html

This majestic Queen Anne home, enthusiastically restored, draws many architecture aficionados. Originally built in 1906 as a private residence, it is considered one of a kind in the historic Irvington District, an area known for its show of uniquely different styles of home design. Inside and out, this particular showcase is elaborate, rich with many of the English and medieval touches that became so popular with William Morris and the Arts and Crafts movement. Downstairs the public spaces are immense, with oversized antique furniture and an abundance of Victoriana in deep, dark tones. Guests are invited to roam at will through these rooms. Even the kitchen is open to your comings and goings. Light refreshments are served every afternoon and Steve and Dusty, the innkeepers, are happy to share their knowledge about the house and the local area. Upstairs wide, carpeted hallways extend to the bedrooms. The Lavonna Room is one of the most popular because of its distinctive round cupola setting. In Starina, the circa-1860 high-back Edwardian bed with matching furniture is great fun to experience! All rooms are equipped with phones, data ports, WiFi and cable TV. Located near the MAX light rail transit. Only five minutes from the Convention Center and two blocks from good restaurants. *Directions:* From I-5, take exit 302-A . Turn onto NE Weidler, left on NE 15th Ave, cross Broadway, and go to the corner of NE Schuyler.

LION AND THE ROSE VICTORIAN INN
Innkeepers: Steve Unger & Dustin Carsey
1810 NE 15th Avenue
Portland, OR 97212, USA
Tel: (503) 287-9245, Fax: (503) 287-9247
Toll Free: (800) 955-1647
6 Rooms, Double: $149–$179
Open: all year, Credit cards: all major
www.karenbrown.com/lionandrose.html

One word comes immediately to mind the moment you step through the front mahogany doors and into the impressive foyer of Portland's White House: opulence. You'll be welcomed warmly at the foot of a sweeping, central staircase below antique, stained-glass windows, knowing full well you are in no ordinary place and in for no ordinary experience. Pure elegance describes this gorgeously restored Colonial Revival Mediterranean-styled mansion, graced in front by a circular drive and classic Greek columns. Notice the exquisite use of color throughout the public rooms downstairs and the original hand-painted French wallpaper with mahogany trim. An antique porcelain collection lines the game room, while a crystal chandelier commands attention in the dining room. There are five marvelous bedrooms in the main building and three in the neighboring Carriage House. All feature feather beds, private baths, air conditioning, flat-screen TV/DVD, CD players, telephones, data ports and wireless internet . A full gourmet breakfast is served at an elegant table in the formal dining room. Majestic, presidential, and thoroughly romantic, Portland's White House will leave its impression long after you've reluctantly walked away. *Directions:* From I-5 south, take the Lloyd Center/ Rose Garden Exit to the second stoplight. Turn left on Weidler and left again on NE 22nd Avenue.

PORTLAND'S WHITE HOUSE
Innkeepers: Lanning Blanks & Steve Holden
1914 NE 22nd Street
Portland, OR 97212, USA
Tel: (503) 287-7131, Fax: (503) 249-1641
Toll Free: (800) 272-7131
8 Rooms, Double: $125–$225
Open: all year, Credit cards: all major
www.karenbrown.com/portlandwhite.html

Many visitors come to this North Umpqua paradise for some of the best fly-fishing in the world, but anyone venturing this way will be richly rewarded. The setting is spectacular: lush, fragrant, cool, unspoiled, with the crashing of the mighty river to overtake your senses. Several types of accommodations are available, all sophisticatedly simple. Below the main building sit eight Streamside Cabins that share a common veranda. Moderate in size, pine-paneled, and handsomely appointed, they are exhilaratingly close to the river. We stayed in one of the Hideaway Cottages about half a mile upriver in a very private setting. Cottages come with a mini-kitchen, king bed, tiled soaking tub/shower, a wood-burning fireplace, and an upstairs loft with twin beds. River Suites are like small homes and offer river views and privacy. The Steamboat is well known for is its evening meal. It begins in the garden-view library where hors d'oeuvres and complimentary wines are served and guests have a chance to mingle. After a while, all are escorted to the lobby area to take a seat at one massive, wood table set beautifully with candles and fresh flowers. Our dinner was exceptional: buttery Chinook salmon, fresh vegetables, roasted potatoes, bread warm from the oven and great conversation. In season, breakfast and lunch are also served in the dining area. *Directions:* On Hwy 138, 45 minutes northeast of Roseburg. Watch for signs.

STEAMBOAT INN
Owners: Jim & Sharon Van Loan, Manager: Patricia Lee
42705 North Umpqua Hwy
Steamboat, OR 97447, USA
Tel: (541) 498-2230, Fax: (541) 498-2411
Toll Free: (800) 840-8825
20 Rooms, Double: $160–$280*
*Breakfast not included: $8.50-11
All meals offered in high season
Open: Mar 1 to Dec 31, Credit cards: MC, VS
www.karenbrown.com/steamboat.html

Here's a lovely resting spot only 100 feet from the ocean and 7 miles south of the town of Yachats. It's quiet, comfy, and romantic, and you'll feel the tension ease as soon as you climb the carpeted stairs to the Great Room. Oversized couches and chairs are arranged in such a way that you can easily find a corner of your own: in front of the wood-burning brick fireplace, in front of the windows overlooking the water, or in any number of nooks and crannies. Decorated in colorful plaids and florals, and carpeted throughout, it's bright and cheerful with lots of huge windows and skylights. Pictures and paintings occupy every space on the large walls. Classical music is piped in and something delectable, like pound cake with lemon curd, is left out for you to enjoy with a cup of tea. A separate library downstairs offers another place to get away. It feels wonderfully secluded, with low wood ceilings and a wet bar nearby. Binoculars are supplied so you can wander onto the deck and watch migrating whales go by. Guestrooms are very private, each with its own entrance and balcony. They feature gorgeous beds with lavish fabrics and lots of extra pillows, comfortable sitting chairs, beautifully tiled bathrooms with Jacuzzi tubs, and stunning ocean views. The "five-star" breakfast buffet is laid out on a beautifully tiled, open kitchen counter in the Great Room. *Directions:* Seven miles south of Yachats' town center, right off Hwy 101.

SEA QUEST INN BED & BREAKFAST
Innkeepers: Kelley & Gabe Essoe
95354 Hwy 101
Yachats, OR 97498, USA
Tel: (541) 547-3782, Fax: none
Toll Free: (800) 341-4878
7 Rooms, Double: $170–$350
Open: all year, Credit cards: all major
www.karenbrown.com/seaquest.html

Places to Stay
Washington

151

There are innkeepers and there are innkeepers, but Joan and Al Waters rank among the most genuine you'll have the good fortune to meet. Their mansion—a beautiful Queen Ann Victorian—was built in 1905, complete with top-floor game room. Original, leaded windows and exquisite woodwork are in evidence throughout. Common rooms are decorated sparingly in period furnishings. Joan's artistic sense has been put to good use in her choice of colors for the bedrooms, adding contemporary warmth. Captain Gray was our favorite, painted in a handsome shade of green with a beautiful bay window and one wall of 15th-century sailing ships silk-screened on priceless wallpaper. Aunt Gert's Parlor is painted in a handsome forest green. The Master Suite is painted in a traditional Victorian mauve and green. An excellent breakfast is served in the elegant dining room in front of a wood-burning fire, where the table is decorated with fresh flowers and candles. *Directions:* Head west on Wishkaw, turn right on Broadway, left on 5th, and proceed to M Street. Head east on Simpson, turn left on Williams, and proceed to the corner of 5th and M Streets.

ABERDEEN MANSION
Innkeepers: Al & Joan Waters
807 North M Street
Aberdeen, WA 98520, USA
Tel: (360) 533-7079, Fax: none
Toll Free: (888) 533-7079
3 Rooms, Double: $110–$175
Open: all year, Credit cards: all major
www.karenbrown.com/aberdeen.html

Set on the north shore of Hood Canal is Selah Inn's main house with its cedar shake exterior, broad porch, and dormer windows. This custom-built bed and breakfast has a distinctly northwest theme, as displayed in its salmon carvings on the wall and lovely river-rock fireplace. Public areas are small, but handsomely decorated. Upstairs, four guestrooms offer top-quality king- or queen-sized beds covered in luxurious linens and rich fabrics. What really stopped us in our tracks, though, was the option to take rooms in the separate Canal House, a huge two-story, three-bedroom home situated right on the canal with access to 450 feet of waterfront, including a private rocky beach loaded with oysters and clams. Downstairs, enjoy a beautiful river-rock fireplace, a 180-degree view of Hood Canal, a covered deck with hot tub, and access to a large, open kitchen. Three bedrooms upstairs are perfectly appointed. The Beach Suite is the largest, with sliding glass doors opening onto a private deck, a king-sized bed, fireplace, and a step-up, jetted tub for two. Bonnie serves gourmet breakfasts in the main house, as well as a five-course dinner upon request. Much humbler cottages are also available. *Directions:* From I-5 at Tacoma, take Hwy 16 north then take the overpass to Hwy 3 west. Upon entering Belfair, turn right on Hwy 300 and follow it for 3½ miles. Pass Belfair State Park, go left after the inn's signage onto NE Beck, and follow signs, turn left onto Dulalip Landing.

SELAH INN ON HOOD CANAL
Innkeepers: Bonnie & Pat McCullough
NE 130 Dulalip Landing
Belfair, WA 98528, USA
Tel: (360) 275-0916, Fax: (360) 277-3187
Toll Free: (877) 232-7941
7 Rooms, Double: $105–$225
3 cottages: $170–$200*
*Breakfast not included if staying in cottages: $7.50
Open: all year, Credit cards: MC, VS
www.karenbrown.com/selah.html

No number of superlatives could possibly do justice to this amazing luxury hotel. It's everything the most gracefully extravagant residential home might be, and we have yet to see a staff more professional, more delightful, and more committed to protecting the privacy of their guests. Rooms, all with high-speed wireless internet access, are sumptuously appointed with handcrafted cherrywood furniture, gorgeous fabrics, and original art. A marble, limestone, and granite bathroom is graced with a deep soaking tub and a glass-enclosed shower. Your king bed is covered in Indian cotton sheets; your pillows are goose-down. The Bellevue is also a superb athletic club (hence the free weights in your room). This is an extravagant, world-class facility, where hotel guests can take advantage of an outdoor and two indoor pools, an indoor running track, pilates, racquetball, and squash. Treat yourself to the full-service spa. Keep in mind, though, that at no time as a hotel guest will you be even remotely aware that there is an athletic club nearby, so deftly are these two environments kept separate. Dine in any of three restaurants, including the lavish Polaris or the informal café Splash. Another bonus: the hotel offers substantial discounts at the weekend. This hotel is superb. *Directions:* From Seattle, take I-5 to 90 east to 405 north. At Exit 12, turn left on SE 8th Street, right on 114th Ave SE, then left on SE 6th Street. The hotel is on the right.

BELLEVUE CLUB HOTEL
Manager: Matt Hagerman
11200 SE 6th
Bellevue, WA 98004, USA
Tel: (425) 454-4424, Fax: (425) 688-3197
Toll Free: (800) 579-1110
67 Rooms, Double: $175–$1450*
*Breakfast not included: $8
Open: all year, Credit cards: all major
www.karenbrown.com/bellevue.html

The Chrysalis Inn & Spa, situated on Bellingham Bay just blocks from the historic Fairhaven district, is a beautifully decorated and well-appointed boutique hotel with a fine wine library-bar, restaurant and an excellent spa. A large freestanding spiral staircase dominates the high-ceilinged lobby. A gorgeously elegant and contemporary sitting area overlooks the bay with wood-burning fireplace, fresh flower arrangements, many richly colored oil paintings and other pieces of fine art, and beautiful Japanese-style light fixtures. Guestrooms are spacious and artfully composed, blending slate floors with carpet, balancing wood with fabrics in subtly metallic shades of brown, purple, silver, green, and gold. All have either whole or partial views of the activity on Bellingham Bay, including ferries sailing to and from Victoria and the San Juan Islands. All offer window seats with Roman blinds, double soaking or whirlpool tubs, glass showers, and every other amenity you'd expect in a modern hotel. A full hot breakfast is served buffet-style in the strikingly attractive Fino Wine Bar, which is also open for lunch and dinner. The hotel spa is top of the line, decorated in soothing Japanese-style elegance. Occasional trains pass by on the tracks in front of the inn. *Directions:* Leave I-5 north at Old Fairhaven and turn left. Turn right on 12th, left on Taylor, right on 10th.

❄ ☕ ⚒ 💳 ☎ 🛗 🍸 P 🍽 ❀ ♿ ✝ 🏌 👫 🎿 ⚓ ⛹

CHRYSALIS INN & SPA AT THE PIER
Innkeeper: Mike Keenan
804 10th Street
Bellingham, WA 98225, USA
Tel: (360) 756-1005, Fax: (360) 647-0342
Toll Free: (888) 808-0005
43 Rooms, Double: $199–$289
Open: all year, Credit cards: all major
Select Registry
www.karenbrown.com/chrysalis.html

Schnauzer Crossing is the delightful and creatively contemporary home of two of the most charming hosts anywhere (including, of course, Marika and Klipsun the schnauzers). Enter a cathedral-like space bordered by sets of wood-framed glass doors that open onto a wraparound deck overlooking Lake Whatcom and Monty's exquisite garden. Add a 20-foot window at the far end of the room and an A-framed ceiling of glass over the dining table, and you get a marvelous living space designed to bring the outside in. Wander the grounds outside and enjoy the aviary, the Zen garden, the outdoor hot tub and the koi pond. Inside the main house, two very different spaces are available. A small, but thoroughly charming, Queen Room offers a lovely view of the lake. Its bathroom is situated right outside the door in a private hallway. In the spacious Garden Suite, wraparound windows take full advantage of lush surroundings. This room offers a marvelous, sunny, sitting room, a wood-burning fireplace, and a large bathroom with Jacuzzi tub and shower. For ultimate privacy, The Cottage is a wonderful space. *Directions:* Leave I-5 north at Exit 253, turning right at the end of the off-ramp (King). Turn left on Lakeway Drive, go up the hill 2-8/10 miles; and immediately after Euclid, fork left on Lakeway Drive, then turn left again at the well-posted inn sign.

SCHNAUZER CROSSING
Innkeepers: Donna & Monty McAllister
4421 Lakeway Drive
Bellingham, WA 98229, USA
Tel & Fax: (360) 734-2808
Toll Free: (800) 562-2808
2 Rooms, Double: $150–$275
1 cottage
Open: all year, Credit cards: MC, VS
www.karenbrown.com/schnauzer.html

This is a wonderful retreat nestled in 6 wooded acres along the shores of gentle Point Orchard Bay, with lovely grounds enhanced by an attractive water feature encompassing three ponds The main house, built in 1926, offers five comfortable rooms to suit every taste. We liked the Tower Suite best, in cool shades of blue and white, with a private balcony overlooking the bay, queen bed set under a high-ceilinged turret, and stained-glass. Bunking in The Penthouse is like living in a daydream: one enormous room, something like a loft with a turreted ceiling and large windows on three sides, decorated with a sense of humor in safari themes. From it, the views of water, forest, and orchard are inspiring. On the ground floor, the Library Room has a spectacular bathroom across the hall with its own sauna. For families, the casual Beach House is a great private space: a three-bedroom vacation home with full kitchen and hot tub. There's also The Hill House, retaining every bit of its 1918 rustic charm, with fireplace, sunroom, full kitchen, and whirlpool tub. Or try The Gatehouse, high up on the hill, with a two-person swing on the porch and full kitchen. Whichever spot you choose, this is an informally elegant, low-key environment where you can count on quiet and the warmest of welcomes. Breakfast and housekeeping are not available in the three cabins. *Directions:* Too complicated to spell out in the space available here! Please call for detailed directions.

ILLAHEE MANOR BED & BREAKFAST AND CABINS
Owner: Austin Case
Innkeepers: Brent & Kim Ewald
6680 Illahee Road NE
Bremerton, WA 98311, USA
Tel: (360) 698-7555, Fax: (360) 698-0688
Toll Free: (800) 693-6680
5 Rooms, Double: $125–$250
3 cabins
Open: all year, Credit cards: all major
www.karenbrown.com/illahee.html

Imagine waking to views of the very spot where Lewis and Clark first reached the Pacific Ocean in 1805. China Beach Retreat is an intimate, three-bedroom hideaway and a very special place. Hardwood floors, low ceilings, leaded stained glass, and eclectic collections of antique furniture characterize the cozy downstairs: sophisticated yet informal, elegant yet rustic. Marvel at the tranquil surroundings through ten huge panes of glass, not a neighbor in sight. The largest bedroom is situated right off the sitting room. It's painted in a cheerful orange sherbet and has its own sun porch with eight windows. A beautiful, wood-framed queen bed sits in the center of the room covered in a rich floral print. Two enchanting rooms upstairs are surrounded on two sides by windows, so you can enjoy the view from your bed. One is papered in a subtle floral of yellow, white, and rose; the other is painted a lovely shade of white-green complemented with dark antique furniture. Both offer large modern baths with handsome tile work. A recent addition is the Audubon Cottage that is separate from the main house and enjoys a private exterior soaking tub. David and Laurie's gourmet breakfasts are served at The Shelburne Inn, about five minutes away. *Directions:* Check in at The Shelburne Inn. Take Hwy 101 north across the Astoria Bridge, turn left to Ilwaco, and drive north 2 miles to Seaview. The Shelburne is at 4415 Pacific Way.

CHINA BEACH RETREAT
Innkeepers: David Campiche & Laurie Anderson
222 Robert Gray Drive
P. O. Box 537
Ilwaco, WA 98624, USA
Tel: (360) 662 5660, Fax: (360) 642-8904
Toll Free: (800) 466-1896
3 Rooms, Double: $199–$229
Cottage: $279
Open: all year, Credit cards: all major
www.karenbrown.com/china.html

La Conner is a charming Victorian village tucked along the edge of the Swinomish Channel in a lush region that boasts the riches of both farming and fishing. Quaint shops and restaurants line the village streets, and the Channel Lodge is the only accommodation in town that takes advantage of the water setting. We provide directions for arrival by car, but you can also tie up your own vessel at the hotel's pierside docks! A long, rambling, three-story building, weathered timbers and shakes dress the front of the lodge's façade. The reception is just off the entry and opposite an intimate lounge set in front of a river-rock fireplace whose chimney climbs to the open second floor landing which opens onto a lovely outdoor deck. Tucked off the lobby is a small sitting area/library whose piano is center stage, enhancing a wine reception hosted Friday and Saturday evenings. Guestrooms, the majority of which enjoy private decks and overlook the water passageway, are attractive in their décor of beiges, blues and exposed woods, and have gas fireplaces. Even the "standard" rooms enjoy a sitting area. Most definitely request a water view, and in warmer months enjoy the parade of boats as they navigate the channel. First floor rooms enjoy access to paths that extend from the private decks. A buffet breakfast is offered on the second floor landing that looks down to the lobby and out through an expanse of window to the channel. *Directions:* Traveling I-5 north from Seattle, take exit 221; south of Vancouver, take exit 230. Head west to La Conner.

❄ ☕ ✄ 💳 ☎ ♨ P 🖼 ☂ 🚶 🏄

CHANNEL LODGE
Manager: Cindy Nelson
205 N. First Street
P.O. Box 573
La Conner, WA 98257, USA
Tel: (360) 466-1500, Fax: (360) 466-1525
Toll Free: (888) 466-4113
40 Rooms, Double: $130–$290
Open: all year, Credit cards: all major
www.karenbrown.com/channellodge.html

For an authentic taste of Bavaria—not kitsch, but the genuine article—treat yourself to a stay at Abendblume Pension, a unique and imposing inn set in a spacious green valley surrounded by mountains. In 1994, Randy and Renee Sexauer transformed their passion for Bavarian architecture and traditions into a luxurious guesthouse experience. You'll notice the stunning staircase railing as soon as you enter: it's the innovative creation of a Czechoslovakian metal artist now living in Leavenworth, and one of many elements of fine artistry and craftsmanship that make this Bavarian dream home so appealing. Look for Randy's handiwork in the gorgeous living-room mantel or in the wood-paneled ceiling in the breakfast room. Guestrooms are radiant and opulent. Whether modest or extravagant, all are open and light with fresh touches of Bavaria you won't see except abroad, like the unique way the comforters are folded. No matter which room you choose, you can't go wrong: feather beds and comforters; fine, ironed linens; beautiful tile work; fresh flowers. Enjoy a European buffet in the morning, complete with muesli, meats, and cheeses, until Renee brings one of her inspired hot dishes to the table. Abendblume achieves the theme approach with taste and style. *Directions:* From Seattle, turn left on Ski Hill off Hwy 2 as you enter Leavenworth. Turn left on Ranger Road.

ABENDBLUME PENSION
Innkeepers: Randy & Renee Sexauer
12570 Ranger Road
P.O. Box 981
Leavenworth, WA 98826, USA
Tel: (509) 548-4059, Fax: none
Toll Free: (800) 669-7634
7 Rooms, Double: $118–$267
Open: all year, Credit cards: all major
www.karenbrown.com/abendblume.html

As you make that last turn up the unpaved road to Mountain Home Lodge, the signpost reads: Welcome. You're 1,000 feet closer to heaven. Brace yourself: you will never want to leave this exceptional inn hidden in its own Alpine valley with humbling views of the Cascade's Stuart Range. In winter months, the lodge is accessible only by snowcat. Park your car in a lot down the hill and leave the rest to the innkeepers, the buoyant Kathy and Brad Schmidt, who will pick you up and transport you (in more ways than one). Winter rates include all meals and the use of traipsing equipment (cross-country skis, snowshoes, sleds). Ten guestrooms and two thoroughly private cabins are warmly appointed in a luxurious, Northwest-lodge decor. They feature handmade quilts, peeled-pine or vine-maple furniture, plush carpets, robes, complimentary port, wireless and a CD player. For an extra charge, treat yourself to a guided snowmobile tour, then return for a soak in the hot tub. Hike as few or as many of the property's 40 miles of trails as you wish. Land one of the Adirondack swings placed in secluded spots throughout the grounds and enjoy the quiet. Come dinnertime, enjoy a three- to four-course meal. Perfection? That's not superlative enough. *Directions:* From Seattle, take Hwy 2 to the bridge over the Wenatchee River. Immediately after the bridge, turn right on East Leavenworth Road, then left on Mountain Home Road.

MOUNTAIN HOME LODGE
Innkeepers: Brad & Kathy Schmidt
Mountain Home Road
P.O. Box 687, Leavenworth, WA 98826, USA
Tel: (509) 548-7077, Fax: (509) 548-5008
Toll Free: (800) 414-2378
10 Rooms, Double: $110–$510
2 cabins
Dinner: one seating nightly by reservation
Open: all year, Credit cards: MC, VS
www.karenbrown.com/mountainhome.html

A few miles beyond the charming Bavarian village is an even more fairy-tale place: a log cabin nestled amid pine and aspen trees against a rugged backdrop of mountains, and one hundred acres of wildlife refuge; whose beauty is enhanced by the sweeping path and mesmerizing sounds of the run of the river. Cozy and intimate, the décor plays on the theme of an alpine hideaway: rich brown, leather sofas and chairs; walls of exposed logs; rough hewn four-poster beds; river rock surrounding both the fireplaces and the Jacuzzi tubs; and folksy clusters of snowshoes, old weathered skis, bikes, birdhouses and country collections. Although the illusion of a mountain décor beautifully compliments the peaceful setting, it is anything but rustic. Think of every luxury provided by the finest hotels and consider them provided—and then all the unbelievable "extras": binoculars to watch the wildlife including osprey, kingfisher, eagles, deer, and coyote; nuts to attract birds and their accompanying song to the privacy of your deck; for the adventurous, snowshoes and bikes; for the reader, neck rolls to enhance the comfort of your porch swing—honestly too many to detail! Just know that Monty and Karen have anticipated your every need and wish, so that you can truly luxuriate in the peacefulness and romance of the setting which is as poetic as its name. *Directions:* Turn off Hwy 20 on the east side of town; just after the bridge turn onto East Leavenworth Road.

❄ ▣ 💳 ☎ Y P 🚭 🖼 🐾 🚶 🏇 ⛷ 🚣 ⚘ 🍇

RUN OF THE RIVER
Innkeepers: Monty & Karen Turner
9308 East Leavenworth Road
P.O. Box 285
Leavenworth, WA 98826, USA
Tel: (509) 548-7171, Fax: (509) 548-7547
Toll Free: (800) 288-6491
6 Rooms, Double: $225–$255
Ravenwood Lodge: $425
Credit cards: all major
www.karenbrown.com/runoftheriver.html

Set in a relaxed residential neighborhood, the Boreas Inn is the quintessential beach house. Built in 1920, its spaces seem deliberately playful in design. Take one section of hallway upstairs, for example: a narrow, 5-foot-high secret passageway that suddenly opens up to reveal an attic-style bedroom (the charming Hideaway) with dormered ceilings, and beautiful quilt and tile work. The entire place is rather joyously decorated to capture the casual, buoyant nature of living so close to the water. It's intimate, eclectic—a Key West meets the Northwest type of place. The Dunes Suite downstairs is sunny and warm with a beautiful spa-like bathroom under a skylight. French doors open onto a small deck. The Pacifica with its ocean view is especially inviting in its cool blues and whites. Wander a five-minute, Hobbit-like path down to the beach. Soak in the hot tub out in a private gazebo. A sunny, casual sitting room with chenille loveseats, fireplace and large windows offers many amusements. For a trip back to San Francisco's Summer of Love, rent the funky, neighboring Beach House (breakfast not included), a 120-year-old, three-bedroom cottage with uneven wooden floors painted in forest green, a brick fireplace, and lots of wicker furniture. Your hosts, Susie and Bill who create award winning breakfasts, could not be more delightful or less intrusive. *Directions:* Driving north on Hwy 101, cross the Astoria Bridge and continue to Long Beach on the 103.

BOREAS BED & BREAKFAST INN
Innkeepers: Susie Goldsmith & Bill Verner
607 N. Ocean Beach Boulevard
P.O. Box 1344
Long Beach, WA 98631, USA
Tel: (360) 642-8069, Fax: (360) 642-5353
Toll Free: (888) 642-8069
5 Rooms, Double: $160–$170
Beach House: $140 per night, $925 per week
Open: all year, Credit cards: all major
www.karenbrown.com/boreas.html

Situated within easy walking distance of the shops, restaurants, and art galleries of Lopez Village, Edenwild is a warmly elegant spot and a good home-base choice for your stay on the island. This two-level, Victorian-style house with wide, wraparound porch and garden pergola, so gracious in light green with white trim, was built in 1990. The downstairs sitting room is comfortable, with a large brick fireplace and plenty of leather couches and chairs, but the real pleasure here awaits in the rooms upstairs. All types are available, depending on your desire. Some have views of the boating activity on Fisherman's Bay, others of the garden. Some have bay windows, others have private entrances. Still others have wood-burning fireplaces, but all are beautifully decorated in rich colors and lovely contemporary fabrics. Attention to luxurious detail is evident throughout the inn, whether it's in-room sherry and chocolates or the innkeepers' original and eclectic art collection. *Directions:* From the ferry, keep straight (Ferry Road, which becomes Fisherman Bay Road). Continue to the village, then turn right on Lopez Road—the inn is on the right.

EDENWILD . . . A COUNTRY INN
Innkeepers: Kris & Robert
132 Lopez Road
P.O. Box 271
Lopez Island—Lopez, WA 98261, USA
Tel & Fax: (360) 468-3238
Toll Free: (800) 606-0662
8 Rooms, Double: $130–$175
Open: all year, Credit cards: MC, VS
www.karenbrown.com/edenwild.html

This is a find: ten handsomely appointed, self-sufficient cottages, each measuring 600 square feet and offering the best of nature and civilization in one perfectly crafted package. Simple and private, painted in rustic burgundy red with a green door and white trim, each is uniquely and artistically designed inside. One might feature traditional furniture in masculine, earthy tones with Tiffany lamps and leather to accent. Another might be bright and sunny with wicker and fabrics of yellows and blues. All have a decidedly sophisticated flair. They are light, open, and airy, with high-quality feather beds, hand-pressed linens, down comforters, gas fireplaces, lush carpets, and built-in breakfast nooks. The kitchens are right out of Williams and Sonoma with a wonderful array of utensils. Stroll over to the herb garden with clippers and help yourself. Wander to the front office and buy a bottle of wine or champagne to sip while you enjoy the amazing colors of the Pacific sunsets sitting in Blackwood's signature Adirondack chairs! If you absolutely must make a phone call or access the internet, a small on-site cabin has been reserved for just those purposes. *Directions:* Driving north on Hwy 101 after the Astoria Bridge, pass through Chinook to Ilwaco, turn north for 2 miles to Seaview, and continue for 8-3/10 miles. The cottages are on your left.

BLACKWOOD BEACH COTTAGES
Innkeepers: James & Peggy Bleckov
20711 Pacific Way
Ocean Park, WA 98640, USA
Tel: (360) 665-6356, Fax: (360) 665-0191
Toll Free: (888) 376-6356
Double: $100–$209*
10 cottages
*Breakfast not included
Open: all year, Credit cards: MC, VS
www.karenbrown.com/blackwood.html

Bob and Marilyn Caswell designed this Queen Ann-style home to serve as an inn. It's set at the edge of Willapa Bay on five lush acres of land overlooking "the other" Long Island (home only to a national wildlife refuge), a series of oyster beds, and the gentle coastal range. The place feels very new and modern. Except for burgundy carpeting in many of the common areas, white is the dominant theme. In the central sitting area, graced by white couches around a white fireplace, high ceilings and large windows keep the focus on the world outside. Breakfast is served family style at a large table in the dining room adjacent to a sun porch overlooking the bay (the spot to witness the spectacular sunsets). Fresh, local oysters are part of every breakfast menu. Guestrooms are available in various sizes, but all are designed to showcase the Caswells' impressive collection of antique bedroom furniture. The Shoal Water features a stunning three-piece walnut set, complete with marble-top nightstands and accented with handsome Eastlake chairs. Even a cozy room like Garden boasts a beautiful honey-oak bed frame dating from 1890, with Lincoln rockers to complement. All are light and bright. *Directions:* Driving north on Hwy 101 after the Astoria Bridge, pass through Chinook to Ilwaco. At the traffic light in Ilwaco, turn right and travel north to Ocean Park. Turn right on Bay Avenue, then right on Sandridge Road. The inn is on the left in half a mile.

CASWELL'S ON THE BAY
Innkeepers: Bob & Marilyn Caswell
25204 Sandridge Road
Ocean Park, WA 98640, USA
Tel: (360) 665-6535, Fax: (360) 665-6500
Toll Free: (888) 553-2319
5 Rooms, Double: $140–$190
Open: all year, Credit cards: all major
www.karenbrown.com/caswells.html

Charles Nelson was an oysterman, and a cranberry man. Born and raised in nearby Oysterville, in 1929 he decided to build his wife a house on the shores of Willapa Bay, so he ordered a Dutch Colonial from a Sears and Roebuck catalogue like any fine young gentleman might. The outcome is a beautiful gray-shingled house that has perfectly withstood the test of time. There are windows absolutely everywhere. It's cheerful, clean, and light in a kind of Norman Rockwell way. Ginger and Curt have painted the entryway a welcoming shade of blue, which looks great against the hardwood floors, the throws, and the quilts on the wall. The surrounding common rooms are small, but inviting, especially the sun porch overlooking the water and garden. Our favorite guestrooms were Charlie's Room overlooking the bay through several windows at the foot of the bed; and Nancy's Room, decorated in a sunny, country style with cheerful yellows, blues, and whites. Its windows overlook the garden. The most popular feature in Elsa's Room, the largest, is the bathroom; daringly outfitted with the original lavender toilet, tub, and pedestal sink. *Directions:* Driving north on Hwy 101 after the Astoria Bridge, pass through Chinook to Ilwaco. At the traffic light in Ilwaco, turn right and travel north to Ocean Park. Turn right on Bay Avenue—the inn is on the corner at Sandridge.

CHARLES NELSON GUEST HOUSE
Innkeepers: Ginger & Curt Bish
26205 Sandridge Road
Ocean Park, WA 98640, USA
Tel: (360) 665-3016, Fax: (360) 665-5962
Toll Free: (888) 826-9756
3 Rooms, Double: $150–$170
Open: all year, Credit cards: all major
www.karenbrown.com/charlesnelson.html

Located on the sunny north shore of Lake Quinault this is a terrific alternative to the Lake Quinault Lodge. Accommodations offered include nine comfortable lakeside units and two lavish, creekside cabins—all enjoying stellar views of the lake and surrounds. Set on 5½ acres of private land right inside Olympic National Park, the resort serves as a great base camp for exploring the entire peninsula and is ideally located at the northernmost start of a scenic 30-mile loop around the lake (our favorite in the park for viewing rain forest and river habitats). Bask in the sun on the beach or simply recline in one of the Adirondack chairs that line the 200-foot trellis covered deck. The deck—a "24-hour quiet zone"—is a very welcoming spot to unwind, with plants and flowers everywhere. Rooms in the original section exude a rustic charm. Unit 8, for example, boasts original knotty-pine walls, French doors that lead into the cozy bedroom and a tiny kitchen with pink linoleum counters. In summer months guests enjoy campfires on the beach. There is a 24-foot pontoon boat that will take you out on the glittering lake twice a day, including a sunset cruise. You'll find a horseshoe pit, a barbecue gazebo, a picnic table, and lots of lush lawn space. The focus remains on the extraordinary beauty of this corner of rain-forest wilderness. *Directions:* Located at the south end of Olympic, off Hwy 101 in Olympic National Park. Signposted on the north shore of Lake Crescent.

LAKE QUINAULT RESORT
Innkeepers: Jon Hawkins & Family
314 North Shore Road
Amanda Park, Lake Quinault
Olympic National Park–Amanda Park, WA 98526, USA
Tel: (360) 288-2362, Fax: (360) 288-2218
Toll Free: (800) 650-2362
9 Rooms, Double: $129–$169*
*Breakfast not included
Open: all year, Credit cards: all major
www.karenbrown.com/lakequinault.html

When one thinks of the Olympic National Park, what comes immediately to mind are its breathtaking rain forests with sunlight filtering through towering trees, cascading waterfalls, and the ground carpeted with giant ferns. However, the park also includes land tracing the Pacific coastline where you find a different type of spectacular scenery. If you love the rugged, wild beauty of pristine, windswept beaches, the Kalaloch Lodge is a great choice for a place to stay. The hotel is perched on a bluff overlooking the ocean where the Kalaloch Creek joins the sea and has deposited huge trees carried down from the rain forests. The hotel dates back to the early 1920s (before there was any road access) when Charles Becker built a simple hotel and cabins here to accommodate hearty tourists. Although renovated over the years, the lodge still exudes old-world charm; the exterior is clad in weathered shingles enhanced by windows and doors trimmed in blue. Inside, the décor is quite simple. There is a cute gift shop, a basic lounge, and a large dining room with windows overlooking the sea. Some of the guest rooms are in the main building, others are in simple cabins that are stretched along the bluff—if you like nature at its finest, ask for one of the front row cabins with the best view. If you choose the Kalaloch Lodge, be sure to visit the nearby Ruby Beach—a place of unbelievable natural grandeur. *Directions:* Located on Hwy 101, on the sea, 35 miles southwest of Forks.

KALALOCH LODGE
Manager: Vickie Williams
157151 Highway 101, Forks
Olympic National Park–Kalaloch, WA 98331, USA
Tel: (360) 962-2271, Fax: (360) 962-3391
Toll Free: (866) 525-2562
64 Rooms, Double: $139–$269*
*Breakfast not included
Open: all year, Credit cards: all major
www.karenbrown.com/kalalochlodge.html

As a base for exploring and savoring the wonders of the breathtaking Olympic National Park, the Lake Crescent Lodge cannot be surpassed. In every respect, this hotel is a real jewel. It has a prime location right on the edge of the stunning Lake Crescent wrapped by layers of mountains. On calm days, the lake's still waters are reminiscent of the majestic fjords of Norway. The heart of the hotel is an appealing, old-fashioned, white wood-frame building with an old-fashioned porch in front where guests relax in rocking chairs and enjoy an idyllic view across a lawn to the shore where rowboats dot the pebbled beach and a pier stretches into the water. The oldest part of the hotel dates back to 1916 when one of the early settlers, Al Singer, operated a tavern here. The nostalgic charm is felt throughout. A spacious lounge has an inviting ambiance with paneled walls, hardwood floors, a bar in one corner, and a stone fireplace adorned with a stag. A few of the least-expensive guestrooms (without private bathrooms) are in this part of the hotel. The most sought after accommodations are the Roosevelt Cottages with stone fireplaces. Stretching along the edge of the lake, these cottages were built in 1937 to commemorate the visit of Franklin Roosevelt. In addition, a wide variety of other types of rooms are located in newer annexes and are more contemporary in mood. *Directions:* Located at the north end the park, off Hwy 101. Signposted on the south shore of Lake Crescent.

LAKE CRESCENT LODGE
Manager: Gary Wood
416 Lake Crescent Road
Olympic National Park-Port Angeles, WA 98363, USA
Tel: (360) 928-3211, Fax: (360) 928-3253
52 Rooms, Double: $82–$195*
*Breakfast not included
Open: beg-May to mid-Oct, Credit cards: all major
www.karenbrown.com/crescentlodge.html

The Lake Quinault Lodge is a picturesque hotel that has a superb location facing beautiful Lake Quinault. The hotel is appealing from the moment you see the two-story building clad in brown wood shingles that are highlighted by windows with white trim framed by bright green shutters. To complete the scene, a few cute gabled windows peek out from a steeply pitched roof that is topped by a wrought-iron weather vane of an Indian chief shooting a mountain lion. Built in 1926 by some of the finest artisans in the Pacific Northwest, the lodge is similar to some other famous park lodges built in the same era such as Old Faithful Lodge in Yellowstone. When you enter, the spacious, rustic-style, wood-paneled lounge is exceptionally attractive with a beamed ceiling, a large brick fireplace, and light streaming in through floor to ceiling windows on facing walls. The dining room too is a winner with windows looking out to the lake. The best feature is not revealed until you walk out the back and discover a lovely view overlooking the lake, and lawn chairs dotting an expansive lawn that sweeps down to the water's edge where there is a pebbly beach, a boat dock and white gazebo. Some of the guestrooms are in the main building, others are in separate buildings. Our favorite accommodations are in the Fireplace building (such as room 230 or 232); these have fireplaces to keep warm on chilly evenings and balconies with pretty lake views. *Directions:* Located at the south end of the park off Hwy 101.

LAKE QUINAULT LODGE
Manager: Charles Willis
Lake Quinault
Olympic National Park
Lake Quinault, WA 98575, USA
Tel & Fax: (360) 288-2900
Toll Free: (800) 562-6672
92 Rooms, Double: $117–$255*
*Breakfast not included
Open: all year, Credit cards: all major
www.karenbrown.com/lakequinaultlodge.html

For a real island adventure, consider one of Jennifer Fralick's cabins on Orcas Island. Found in four different locations, from waterfront cozy to spacious mountain retreat, all are simply, but fully appointed; have excellently equipped kitchens; and are an integral part of their environments. You'll feel positively enveloped in nature. Cabins-on-the-Point is situated on 3 acres of alternately manicured lawn-garden and raw wilderness. The Heather Cabin is balanced so close to the water's edge, you might be tempted to dive from the windows right into the bay. Nearly a hundred years old, it is very small but completely inviting. The bedroom's greatest asset is a three-sided bay window nook, just barely big enough for the queen-sized bed snuggled perfectly into it. In the body of the cabin there's a captain's bed, such as you might find on a ship, tucked directly under a window; plus cozy sitting chairs, a stone fireplace, a small dining table, and a wee kitchen. The Primrose Cabin is a converted bunkhouse with low ceilings, skylights, and lots of windows. Hidden in a grove of trees, it has a queen bed, a wood-burning stove, a step-down kitchen, and a small bath with shower. Both these cabins share an outdoor hot tub set under a canopy of tall trees, out near the water's edge. Whichever location you choose, you are in for a real treat. *Directions:* Go left from the ferry ramp for 2½ miles, turn left on Deer Harbor Road, go 2 miles to 2101 on your left.

CABINS-ON-THE-POINT
Innkeeper: Jennifer Fralick
2101 Deer Harbor Road
Orcas Island—Eastsound, WA 98245, USA
Tel: (360) 376-4114, Fax: none
Double: $195–$395*
6 cabins (self catering)
*Breakfast not included
Open: all year, Credit cards: MC, VS
www.karenbrown.com/cabins.html

Situated on 5 green acres close to what was once home to Orcas Island's first fruit-packing company, the Inn at Ship Bay is a wonderful, small complex with new accommodations overlooking restful Ship Bay. Three, two-level shingled buildings, painted to blend with the 1869 vintage farmhouse, call to you from the road. All rooms are modest in size and similarly decorated in contemporary country style with a subtle northwestern twist: gorgeous walls painted in mustard; king-sized, pillow-top beds with fine linens, down comforters, and beautiful quilts; oversized couches in rich fabrics of green, rose and cream; hurricane lamps as lights. All have gas fireplaces, refrigerators, wet bars, sparkling bathrooms, good showers, and very private decks with water views. Ask about the Sunset Suite, which offers the most space. A Continental breakfast is served every morning. At night, saunter over to the restaurant in the wonderfully restored, 130-year-old farmhouse boasting original hammered-tin walls and ceilings, a sun porch, and a patio overlooking the water. The menu features fresh, locally farmed fruits and vegetables—along with sustainably harvested seafoods and antibiotic/hormone-free meats and poultry. *Directions:* Turn left at the exit from the ferry terminal and follow the main road to, and then through, Eastsound towards Moran State Park. Two miles beyond the village, the Inn at Ship Bay is on the right.

INN AT SHIP BAY
Innkeepers: Geddes & Mary Anna Martin
326 Olga Road
Orcas Island—Eastsound, WA 98245, USA
Tel: (360) 376-5886, Fax: none
Toll Free: (877) 276-7296
11 Rooms, Double: $150–$295
Restaurant: closed Thanksgiving to Mar & Mon
Open: all year, Credit cards: MC, VS
www.karenbrown.com/innatshipbay.html

The two most remarkable things about Otters Pond are, without a doubt, its setting and its hot tub. The setting: a thick wood near Moran State Park with a 20-acre pond of protected wetland; complete with visits from eagles, trumpeter swans, wood ducks, and, yes, an otter, who usually shows up around lunchtime looking for duck eggs. The hot tub: a therapeutic sensation, poised at the pond's edge and sheltered inside a Japanese-style "teahouse" with sliding doors, like shoji screens, to open or close—depending on the weather and your desire for privacy. Guests arriving at this French country-style home are supplied with slippers for padding softly on the polished, hardwood floors and Oriental carpets. Guests are encouraged to relax in the sitting room, the cozy library, or on the deck overlooking the pond. The sitting room takes advantage of the pond setting, complete with binoculars and spotting scope. Bedrooms are cheerful, and yet formal, with fresh bouquets, skylights, and views of the pond and surrounding forest. In the morning, your five-course breakfast is served with all the best crystal and sterling silver. *Directions:* From the ferry, turn left and drive to, and through, the village of Eastsound up the hill to the stop sign, then turn right. Nearly 3 miles farther on towards Moran State Park, pass the large pond on the right and turn right on Tomihi Road. Otters Pond is the second property on the right.

OTTERS POND BED & BREAKFAST
Innkeepers: Carl & Susan Silvernail
100 Tomihi Drive
Orcas Island—Eastsound, WA 98245, USA
Tel: (360) 376-8844, Fax: (360) 376-8847
Toll Free: (888) 893-9680
5 Rooms, Double: $140–$195
Open: all year, Credit cards: all major
www.karenbrown.com/otters.html

You'll shift to relaxation mode the minute you arrive at the enchanting Turtleback Farm Inn, set on 80 acres of gentle green pasture to rival any in Ireland. The only sounds are the wind through trees and the bleating of sheep. The main inn is beautifully and meticulously restored to its original Folk National design, painted a handsome hunter green with pale-yellow trim, and clearly the work of fine craftsmen. Guestrooms are elegant, with comfortable couches and rocking chairs, all decorated gracefully in tones of taupe, rose, and green. Bathrooms are immaculate: polished fir floors with matching wainscoting, claw-foot tubs with sunflower shower heads (some have separate showers), pedestal sinks, and some pull-chain toilets. The newer Orchard House is built of cedar to resemble a barn, and sits some distance from the main house. Its four, lovely rooms are very private, self-sufficient suites. As an option in these rooms, breakfast is delivered through "trap" doors, like those in a dumbwaiter, so you don't have to venture out of your room. Turtleback is a working farm, where breakfast eggs are gathered from resident chickens, bed comforters are lined with the wool of resident sheep, and fruit comes from the farm and orchard. *Directions:* From the ferry, head left up the hill for about 3 miles. Turn left on Deer Harbor Road, drive almost 1 mile, and turn right on Crow Valley Road. The inn is on the right after about 2½ miles.

TURTLEBACK FARM INN
Innkeepers: Susan & Bill Fletcher
1981 Crow Valley Road
Orcas Island—Eastsound, WA 98245, USA
Tel: (360) 376-4914, Fax: (360) 376-5329
Toll Free: (800) 376-4914
11 Rooms, Double: $100–$245
Open: all year, Credit cards: all major
Select Registry
www.karenbrown.com/turtleback.html

Included in the price of your stay at Spring Bay is a daily, two-hour kayak trip right out the back door with innkeepers (retired park rangers) Carl Burger and Sandy Playa as guides. Awaken to a Continental breakfast set up just outside your door and an issue of Spring Bay Today, the inn's own newsletter informing you about the morning's agenda: what the weather's like, when to be ready, who your fellow sailors will be. By 8:30, you're off to explore in kayaks, returning to a full brunch at the dining table. Guests look forward to evening refreshments, a waterfront hot tub, and 2½ miles of hiking trails. The inn sits on 57 gorgeously wooded acres; and serves, as Carl puts it, as a "command center" from which to explore the grounds, the adjacent Obstruction Pass State Park, and the island altogether. Over 250 windows and 14-foot ceilings add to the soaring lodge-like nature of the interior. In the downstairs common area, you will find various nooks for reading or enjoying the water view. Guestrooms are sparingly decorated, almost rustically so; but the beds are great, the fire warm, the views inspiring, and your hosts delightful. *Directions:* From the ferry, take Orcas Road and follow signs through Eastsound, Moran State Park, and Olga. Turn left on Pt. Lawrence Road, right on Obstruction Pass Road after ¾ mile, and right on Trailhead after 8/10 mile. After another ¾ mile, go left through the gate on Spring Bay Trail.

❄ ☕ 🎿 CREDIT ☎ 🍷 P 🌱 🎿 ⊤ 🧍 🚶 🐎 🚣 ⛳

SPRING BAY INN ON ORCAS ISLAND
Innkeepers: Carl Burger & Sandy Playa
P. O. Box 97
Orcas Island—Olga, WA 98279, USA
Tel: (360) 376-5531, Fax: (360) 376-2193
5 Rooms, Double: $220–$260
Open: May to Oct, Credit cards: MC, VS
Oct to Apr: rent the entire inn with dinner, $1000/night
www.karenbrown.com/springbay.html

Port Angeles may not be a destination spot, but Colette's surely is. It's easily our top pick for the area. From the moment you walk into this exquisite inn, you'll stop breathing until you're reminded to exhale! Enter a gorgeous sitting room with a 40-foot wall of windows overlooking a wide expanse of lawn, wood, garden, and the vast Strait of Juan de Fuca. Handsome, comfortable, contemporary furniture around the fireplace includes a brown leather couch and sitting chairs in fabrics of sage. Even the common bathroom off the entryway is artwork, with richly painted burgundy walls and a slated floor. Notice the tiles on this floor, beautifully etched with animal images. On the stone patio, Adirondack chairs encircle an outdoor fireplace. Each bedroom is remarkable. As intimate as they are elegant, as luxurious as they are subtle, not one room in the place will do less than thrill. All promise a superb view, king-sized feather bed, gas fireplace, immaculate spa-like bathroom with two-person Jacuzzi tub, TV/VCR/CD player, and telephone. A gourmet breakfast is served with a view at two large, formal tables. From anywhere on the property, inside or out, enjoy spectacular sunsets that bring on the lights of Victoria from across the strait. *Directions:* Take Hwy 101 west. Three miles past Sequim, turn right on Carlsborg. After 1-8/10 miles, turn left on Old Olympic Hwy, go 3-7/10 miles, and turn right on Matson then left on Finn Hall. Colette's is in one mile.

COLETTE'S BED & BREAKFAST – Cover Painting
Innkeepers: Lynda & Peter Clark
339 Finn Hall Road
Port Angeles, WA 98362, USA
Tel: (360) 457-9197, Fax: (360) 452-0711
Toll Free: (877) 457-9777
5 Rooms, Double: $175–$375
Open: all year, Credit cards: MC, VS
Select Registry
www.karenbrown.com/colettes.html

Domaine Madeleine was the first inn to open on this particular stretch of bluff side Port Angeles. Highlighted by Sunset Magazine, which rated it one of the 20 best seaside getaways in the Northwest, it offers breathtaking views, exquisite gardens, and excellent service. Breakfasts, served at a formal dining table overlooking the water and prepared by excellent resident chefs, are very impressive. Built in 1946 with low ceilings and hardwood floors, the home was remodeled in the early '80s. Furniture and decor lend a feeling of home and bedrooms are supplied with extras that anticipate your every need including designer robes and French perfumes. Guests of The Renoir Suite enjoy use of a large, adjacent Oriental-themed living room with a huge 14-foot basalt fireplace and enormous windows that frame the surrounding views. The room is filled with the owner's personal treasures, including a fine Chinese corner chest. The Ming Suite occupies the entire second floor and has a large, private balcony. For more privacy, the Cottage has its own mini-kitchen, sitting area, and private garden in sight of the Olympic mountain range. Enjoy the unique gardens: a woodland garden, a rose garden, and the Monet garden. *Directions:* Take Hwy 101 west. Three miles past the first exit to Sequim, turn right on Carlsborg. After 1-8/10 miles turn left on Old Olympic Hwy, go 3-7/10 miles, right on Matson, left on Finn Hall. After 1 mile, go right on Wildflower Lane.

DOMAINE MADELEINE
Innkeeper: Jeri Weinhold
146 Wildflower Lane
Port Angeles, WA 98362, USA
Tel: (360) 457-4174, Fax: (360) 457-3037
Toll Free: (888) 811-8376
5 Rooms, Double: $160–$265
Open: all year, Credit cards: all major
www.karenbrown.com/madeleine.html

If you're looking for the convenience of staying right in the heart of Port Angeles, you could do no better than to book into the Five SeaSuns where your hosts will give you a very cordial welcome. Built in 1926, this Dutch Colonial has been carefully renovated and filled with period furnishings. The living room is light and comfortable with a large gas fireplace and French doors leading out to a columned pergola, where guests like to sit and listen to the waterfall splashing into the fishpond. Guests eat a full, cooked breakfast by candlelight around one large table in the dining room. Bedrooms, all with en suite baths, are named for the seasons (the fifth is Indian Summer) and vary in decor. In the main house they have floral wallpaper and are furnished with antiques such as a brass bed or a marble-topped dressing table. Summer, on the ground floor, has a private porch and a Jacuzzi bath; Winter is the largest room and enjoys a deep soaking tub original to the house; Spring is a small room with a private balcony; Autumn has a lovely view of mountains and water. Indian Summer is a carriage house suite with a modern rustic look. The half-acre of gardens are a delight to sit or stroll in (they will even make you smile): by the roadside you'll find upside-down trees with their roots cascading flowers. *Directions:* Enter Port Angeles from the east, the 101 leaves Front Street near the ferries and goes left at Lincoln. The inn is on the right at the corner of Lincoln and 10th.

FIVE SEASUNS
Innkeepers: Jan & Bob Harbick
1006 S. Lincoln Street
Port Angeles, WA 98362, USA
Tel: (360) 452-8248, Fax: (360) 417-0465
Toll Free: (800) 708-0777
5 Rooms, Double: $95–$155
Open: all year, Credit cards: all major
www.karenbrown.com/fiveseasuns.html

This is Victorian at its best. The James House is one of Port Townsend's best-loved period homes, poised dramatically bluff-side in a residential neighborhood designated a National Historic District for its outstanding show of finely restored Victorians. Whether from the front porch or the third floor, views of the water, the Olympics, the Cascades, and Mount Rainier are breathtaking. We took two rooms at the top: Mount Rainier Suite and Bay. The Rainier Suite has a noble feel, with handsome mahogany bed and dramatic arched windows overlooking the water. The Bay Room, painted in pastel yellows with white trim and pale-blue accents, has a queen feather bed in an Eastlake oak frame, and was a perfect perch from which to watch the boats sail by. All rooms are spacious with excellent beds, lots of windows, and good, though modest, bathrooms. A second-floor Master Suite, with sitting room, fireplace, and private balcony, is especially well done. Notice the architectural artistry: the elaborate staircase; the newel posts; the ceiling medallions; the parquet floors made of individually cut oak, walnut, and cherry; the intricate carving. Door hinges and hardware are ornately carved brass. Most importantly, this is a well-run country inn with a very friendly staff. *Directions:* From the ferry landing, turn right toward town. Go left on Adams, then left on Washington, and up the bluff. The inn is on the right.

JAMES HOUSE
Innkeeper: Carol McGough
1238 Washington
Port Townsend, WA 98368, USA
Tel: (360) 385-1238, Fax: (360) 379-5551
Toll Free: (800) 385-1238
12 Rooms, Double: $150–$250
1 cottage, 1 bungalow, 1 hideaway
Open: all year, Credit cards: all major
www.karenbrown.com/james.html

If you've come to Port Townsend to see the incredible Victorian homes in the Victorian district of this charming Victorian seaport town but prefer not to overnight in anything distinctive or Victorian, try the Ravenscroft Inn. Built as an inn, in the style of a Charleston, South Carolina single house, Ravenscroft offers eight contemporary rooms, most with views of Port Townsend Bay and the mountains beyond. There are four levels in this pleasant home. The best rooms occupy the second floor from the top, especially for the French doors that open onto a huge covered verandah, a great place from which to enjoy the views. The Bay Room provides the best view. Fireside has a wood-burning fireplace that gives the room a fragrant woodsy scent. It's attractively decorated in burgundy and green, and features custom-made fabric incorporating Northwest Indian designs. The Admiralty Suite is light and open with a big bathroom with shower, a separate soaking tub on a step-up platform, and an especially wonderful window seat. The Great Room downstairs is a huge space, where a large fireplace and comfortable sitting chairs share room with four small dining tables and a huge open kitchen fit for a Julia Child cooking show! Garden-level rooms on the floor below entry level are a bargain. *Directions:* From the ferry landing, turn right on Water Street, left on Monroe, then left on Clay, and the inn will be just ahead on the corner of Quincy and Clay.

RAVENSCROFT INN
Innkeepers: Gay & Tim Stover
533 Quincy Street
Port Townsend, WA 98368, USA
Tel: (360) 385-2784, Fax: none
Toll Free: (800) 782-2691
8 Rooms, Double: $94–$200
Open: all year, Credit cards: MC, VS
www.karenbrown.com/ravenscroft.html

At the Highland Inn veteran innkeeper and world traveler Helen King has created an environment at once opulent and subtle. Her two magnificent suites are gorgeously decorated and perfectly appointed. The Whale Watch Suite is a country-French masterpiece, while The Haro Strait Suite is richer and more dramatic—with English antique furnishings and stunning accents from the Orient. You won't want to leave either room, except to wander from the bed to the sitting area in front of the wood-burning fireplace, to the jetted tub, to the steam shower, to the window seat, to the deck. An elegant living area right out of Architectural Digest separates the two suites. Guests are welcome to sit in front of the common fire here, or serve themselves tea or coffee. Breakfast is served either in the dining room or direct to your bedroom. Inside your room, you can dine in the window-seat nook or on the spacious deck. From either spot, you'll be able to hear the whales playing and feeding in waters below. Flawless. Magic. *Directions:* From the ferry, take Spring Street, which veers left and becomes San Juan Valley Road. Turn left on Douglas, right on Bailer Hill, and right on Hannah (nearly a U-turn back up the hill). In 2/10 miles, go left on Hannah and follow the gravel road to 439.

HIGHLAND INN
Innkeeper: Helen King
439 Hannah Road
P.O. Box 135
San Juan Island–Friday Harbor, WA 98250, USA
Tel: (360) 378-9450, Fax: (360) 378-1693
Toll Free: (888) 400-9850
2 Rooms, Double: $200–$275
Closed: Thanksgiving, Credit cards: all major
www.karenbrown.com/highland.html

This lovely property, Inn To The Woods, was transformed from a three-bedroom, ranch-style home into an exclusive island getaway. Surrounded by old-growth forest, this house is set up very much like a home away from home. Beige suede couches are arranged to encourage conversation or just relaxing with a good book. A desktop computer is available so you can access the internet. French doors open onto a deck overlooking Sportsman's Lake. On the side-table are always a supply of brownies or blondies plus all you'll need to make yourself a cup of tea or cocoa. A hot breakfast is served inside or out each morning. All four bedrooms are clean, light, and comfortable with lots of windows. A wall-sized window behind the bed in St. John brings the forest right into the room. The Marilyn Room has an outdoor hot tub on a private deck out under the pine trees. Rooms offer every amenity, including a TV/VCR with cordless headphones. Beds are top of the line, with fine linens and down pillows. The white-painted bathrooms are immaculate. Guests have lovely views of Sportsman Lake through the firs. *Directions:* From the ferry landing, take Spring Street up the hill. Turn right on Blair, left on Guard, and right on Tucker, which soon forks—take the left fork (Roche Harbor Road). Turn right on Elena just past the 4-mile marker and follow signs.

INN TO THE WOODS
Innkeeper: Patrick Boyles
46 Elena Drive
San Juan Island–Friday Harbor, WA 98250, USA
Tel: (360) 378-3367, Toll Free: (888) 522-9626
4 Rooms, Double: $129–$219
Open: all year, Credit cards: all major
www.karenbrown.com/inntothewoods.html

Roche Harbor has become a bustling tourist destination on San Juan Island. In the mid-19th century it was a company town, where Roche Harbor Lime and Cement did a thriving business. Visitors throng here now to enjoy the historic old Hotel de Haro, built in 1886; Our Lady of Good Voyage Chapel, used also as a schoolhouse in 1892 for miners' children; old lime quarry trails; and even a 19th-century mausoleum. They come to partake of a wide variety of waterfront activities, too, including whale watching and kayaking tours. The resort has recently put half a million dollars into renovating the old McMillin home—set high on a hill overlooking the harbor—transforming it into four simply but elegantly appointed suites. Each is modest in size but very private, with wonderful views of Pearl and Henry Islands. Each features a king-sized bed with high-quality linens, hardwood floors, gas fireplace, claw-foot tub for two and separate shower, heated bathroom floors, a TV/VCR, cordless phone, and refrigerator. Walls resemble adobe, handsomely painted in pastel shades of yellow to complement wood furnishings. *Directions:* From the ferry landing, take Spring Street up the hill. Turn right on Blair, left on Guard, and right on Tucker, which soon forks. Take the left fork (Roche Harbor Road), drive to the north of the island, and follow signs.

ROCHE HARBOR
Manager: Brent Snow
PO Box 4001
San Juan Island–Roche Harbor, WA 98250, USA
Tel: (360) 378-2155, Fax: (360) 378-6809
Toll Free: (800) 451-8910
24 Rooms, Double: $89–$425*
9 cottages, 22 condos, 4 carriage houses
*Breakfast not included: $8–$13
Open: all year, Credit cards: all major
www.karenbrown.com/rocheharbor.html

Here is the perfect setting for a Murder Mystery Night. As you wend your way down a single-lane road through a dense green forest, the intrigue begins. Pull up to the Frank Lloyd Wright-styled house and enter the lobby and living room, where you find yourself immersed in period formality and Art Deco design, original parquet floors, burgundy carpets, a huge wood fireplace, and high ceilings. French doors open onto a pink brick patio, a lovely garden, and a trail down to the rocky beach. An intimate dining room sits off the living room with spectacular views of Hood Canal and the Olympic Mountains. A few steps below the first floor, you find a pool table and a video room. Upstairs, there's a library with fireplace and chairs of rich red leather. Guestrooms have changed little since 1939 (many connected by secret passageways behind furtive "extra" doors). Constance's Room is the most elaborate with stunning views, marble Art Deco fireplace, and a bathroom full of period luxuries. Clark Gable, a family friend and frequent visitor, stayed in a cozy room now named for him, with private balcony and small bath with shower. *Directions:* From Poulsbo take Hwy 3 south, exit at Newberry Hill Road. Turn right (west) and travel 3 miles, turn right at Seabeck Hwy. Drive just over 13 miles to Old Holly Hill Road and fork right. Go 200 yards and turn right at the mailboxes on Tekiu Road. After just over a mile, turn left at the cabin and enter via the gatehouse.

WILLCOX HOUSE COUNTRY INN
Innkeepers: Phillip & Cecilia Hughes
2390 Tekiu Road
Seabeck, WA 98380, USA
Tel: (360) 830-4492, Fax: none
Toll Free: (800) 725-9477
5 Rooms, Double: $149–$229
Dinners by reservation only
Open: all year, Credit cards: MC, VS
Select Registry
www.karenbrown.com/willcox.html

The Sultan of Brunei feels so at home at the Alexis that he made several of the rooms his very own. In fact, at his own expense, he completely redecorated them! There's a John Lennon Suite, too—notice the copy of a pen-and-ink self-portrait outside "his" room. However, this is not to say that one must be a celebrity to stay at the Alexis. Oddly, there is nothing about the lobby that indicates how special a place this time-honored hotel really is. It is understated, graceful, refined. Rooms are elegant, in shades of gold, cream, rust, and sage. All are spacious, thoroughly appointed, and very quiet; with traditional fabrics, antiques, and original art. On the "Arlington" side of the building, old apartment units have been converted, some to the most marvelous one- and two-room suites with hardwood floors, brick exposures, full kitchens, and skylights. The Honeymoon Suite is really exceptional: a spa suite with dual showerheads, a king bed, love seat, and many extra-special touches. A private steam room is available to all guests by the hour. You'll also find an art collection by local artists on the public floors and an Aveda day spa. Room service is provided by the adjoining Library Bistro, an intimate restaurant serving contemporary American cuisine. The Bookstore, a popular spot for locals, serves lighter fare. *Directions:* From Seattle airport, take I-5 north to Exit 164/Seneca. Turn right on 4th, left on Union, and left on 1st. The hotel is on the right at the corner of Madison.

ALEXIS HOTEL
Manager: Katharine Dooley
1007 First Avenue
Seattle, WA 98104, USA
Tel: (206) 624-4844, Fax: (206) 621-9009
Toll Free: (800) 426-7033
109 Rooms, Double: $299–$599*
*Breakfast not included: $15
Open: all year, Credit cards: all major
www.karenbrown.com/alexis.html

The Gaslight Inn is a superbly restored, 1906 vintage Craftsman home in Capitol Hill filled with museum-quality Arts and Crafts furniture and stunning works of art. The large entrance hall is your introduction to the spacious public rooms, which gleam with rich oak paneling and are decorated with an interesting mix of animal trophy heads, antiques, Northwest Indian artifacts, and impressive contemporary glass pieces. The dining room, where a continental breakfast is served, has beautiful built-in cupboards and a fine collection of pewter plates. Your challenge will be deciding where to relax: should it be in the living room next to the large oak fireplace, in the parlor, in the library, on the window seat on the landing, or out on the deck overlooking the swimming pool? The bedrooms are accessed up an elegant, wide staircase dominated by a beautiful stained-glass window (one of many in the house). Rooms vary in size and amenities, but all are comfortably furnished with double or queen beds, Arts and Crafts furniture, and color TVs. Bathrooms are well equipped and absolutely gleaming. I loved the sitting room of the suite I saw: it was a real haven with leather armchairs and gas fire. Don't let all this perfection intimidate you, though, for the atmosphere here is relaxed and welcoming. *Directions:* From the airport, take I-5 north to Madison St. Turn right onto Madison, left onto 15th Ave, to the inn on the left.

GASLIGHT INN
Innkeepers: Trevor Logan & Steve Bennett
1727 15th Avenue
Seattle, WA 98122, USA
Tel: (206) 325-3654, Fax: (206) 328-4803
9 Rooms, Double: $88–$158
Open: all year, Credit cards: all major
www.karenbrown.com/gaslightinn.html

What really distinguishes the contemporary Inn at Harbor Steps from other hotels in the downtown area is its position near Elliott Bay, at the base of a 25-story luxury residential high-rise. You'll feel like a local, too, as you find yourself sharing elevators, saunas, and indoor Jacuzzi and resistance pools with these residents, or when wandering out into the wonderfully urban, courtyard garden sequestered between residential towers. Like a posh apartment and a quality hotel all in one, this is an artful modern space adjacent to Seattle's Harbor Steps. Public areas, very spacious and handsomely decorated, are arranged on two floors. Four types of guestrooms are available. The newer ones, with partial views of the water from small balconies, overlook the steps and another high-end residential apartment building. The elevator system to get to these rooms takes some getting used to, however. All rooms have high ceilings and make wonderful use of natural light. Many offer gas fireplaces and roomy bathrooms artistically designed. A Four Sister's Inn, in the afternoons, complimentary tea, wine, cheese, and sweets are offered in the solarium-like library off the garden. A full breakfast is served in the attractive adjoining dining room. Parking is available in the multi-level garage—be sure to drop off your bags first. *Directions:* From Seattle airport, take I-5 north to Exit 164/Seneca. Turn right on 6th, left on Union, and left on 1st. The hotel is on the right after University.

INN AT HARBOR STEPS
Manager: Gregory Crick
1221 First Avenue
Seattle, WA 98101, USA
Tel: (206) 748-0973, Fax: (206) 748-0533
Toll Free: (888) 728-8910
28 Rooms, Double: $175–$275
Open: all year, Credit cards: all major
www.karenbrown.com/harborsteps.html

The acclaimed Inn at Market is JUST the kind of place we like: an independently owned boutique hotel with a marvelous location and friendly staff. And what a location—right in the heart of Seattle behind Pike Place Market, with stunning views of Elliott Bay and the Olympics. Although it is just steps away from so much action, the hotel is buffered from the bustle by a plant-filled, fountain courtyard from which you enter into the stylish lobby with its impressive collection of Northwest art. Guestrooms come in ten categories, with price dependent on the view (water, market, courtyard or city) through floor-to-ceiling windows. They are uniformly decorated with a clean, sophisticated style and a palette of muted colors, which has a very restful effect. The amenities offered are first-class: Tempurpedic mattresses, refrigerators, cable TV with movie system, personal voice mail, modem dataports, and in-room safes, among others. Two deluxe rooms share a balcony. Bathrooms are spacious and well lit and even have a telephone. When it's time to relax, sink into a chair on the fifth-floor deck and soak in the gorgeous water view. Within the courtyard are three places to eat: Bacco, a small café serving breakfast and lunch; the bistro-style Café Campagne; and the award-winning Campagne, offering southern French cuisine. For fun and value, inquire about the packages the hotel offers. *Directions:* On Pine at First Street—the entrance and loading zone are before Post Alley.

INN AT THE MARKET
Manager: Jack Dooley
86 Pine Street
Seattle, WA 98101, USA
Tel: (206) 443-3600, Fax: (206) 448-0631
Toll Free: (800) 446-4484
70 Rooms, Double: $210–$600
Open: all year, Credit cards: all major
www.karenbrown.com/innatmarket.html

How very convenient! When you're feeling exhausted from shopping in the Westlake Center or get off the monorail there after a busy day of sightseeing, you can just stroll across a covered walkway into the delightful Mayflower Park Hotel, and revive yourself with an award-winning martini in the popular Oliver's bar, or retire to your comfortable bedroom. This historic, privately owned hotel is a gracious, tastefully appointed place with a truly wonderful staff and hands-on owners, who are committed to an ongoing program of renovation. In 2001, for example, all the bathrooms were updated with first-class fixtures and had their original, deep soaking tubs reglazed. As soon as you enter the spacious reception area with its antiques, crystal chandelier, and lavish flower arrangements, you are enveloped in an old-world atmosphere of understated elegance and charm. All types of bedrooms are available, including 13 luxury suites. Rooms are individually decorated in a most pleasing traditional style, with rich fabrics used for bedspreads and drapes, and comfortable seating areas. Among its many amenities, the hotel offers high-speed wireless internet access and 24-hour room service from the Andaluca restaurant downstairs. There are many special packages offered throughout the year, which are an excellent value. *Directions:* From Seattle airport, take I-5 north to Seneca Street. Turn right on 4th and the hotel is on the corner of 4th and Olive.

❄ 🚲 💳 ☎ 🛗 🏋 P 🍴 🔔 ⚓ ♿ ✝ 🚶 🎿 ⛷ ⚓

MAYFLOWER PARK HOTEL
Innkeepers: Marie & Bernie Dempcy
405 Olive Way
Seattle, WA 98101, USA
Tel: (206) 623-8700, Fax: (206) 382-6997
Toll Free: (800) 426-5100
171 Rooms, Double: $149–$365*
*Breakfast not included
Open: all year, Credit cards: all major
www.karenbrown.com/mayflower.html

The Hotel Monaco bills itself as pet friendly. If upon arrival you find yourself without such a companion, they'll supply one: a goldfish in a bowl, complete with name tag. If you become especially attached to your goldfish, you may request the same one for your return visits. After passing through the big, blue entry doors, you enter a lobby that is at once Moorish, Mediterranean, and Carnival. The ceiling towers 22 feet above you. A fire glows underneath two enormous, three-tiered chandeliers. Comfortable sitting chairs are arranged throughout in shades of blue and green, gold and rusty red. A large round goldfish bowl rests on the reception counter. One can't help smiling here. The bright and cheerful guestrooms are decorated with the same sense of fun, with striped wallpaper in alternating vertical columns of crimson and gold, where florals mix with stripes mix with patterns, all in vibrant, shameless colors. And we won't even mention the leopard-print bathrobes! All rooms are furnished with private bars, personal fax machines, two-line phones, and CD players, and all have free broadband internet access. An evening wine reception is hosted in the lobby living room. Immediately adjacent to the hotel is the energetic and equally colorful Sazerac restaurant. *Directions:* From Seattle airport, take I-5 north to Exit 164A Dearborn/James/Madison, stay left, turn left on Madison, and right on 4th. The hotel is on the corner of 4th and Spring.

HOTEL MONACO
Director: Jeremy Strober
1101 Fourth Avenue
Seattle, WA 98101, USA
Tel: (206) 621-1770, Fax: (206) 621-7779
Toll Free: (800) 945-2240
189 Rooms, Double: $175–$349*
*Breakfast not included: $15–$20
Open: all year, Credit cards: all major
www.karenbrown.com/monaco.html

Sitting on the corner of a broad, tree-lined street in Capitol Hill, a few blocks from Volunteer Park, Salisbury House offers immaculate accommodation within a beautifully renovated 1904 Prairie-style house. High-ceilinged public rooms with lovely hardwood floors are furnished with great taste and envelop the guest in comfort. The open-plan sitting and dining rooms, with their white-painted woodwork, are light and airy; and well-placed groupings of chairs and sofas encourage guests to relax around the large fireplace. The library across the hall is a cozy spot to sip your morning coffee or play a game of chess. Upstairs, there are four, traditionally furnished, queen bedrooms (all corner rooms) with private bathrooms. Each room has a different color scheme and mood, but all are charming. For example, the Rose room has a canopy bed draped in floral material, antique writing desk, and window seat; while the Lavender room, which can sleep three, offers a mahogany sleigh bed and a 6-foot-long soaking tub. Downstairs, with its entrance off the pretty garden, a spacious suite, more contemporary in decor, has a sitting area with fireplace and TV, a wet bar, and a huge whirlpool tub. All this and the friendliest of innkeepers, too! *Directions:* From Seattle airport, take I-5 north to Madison St. Turn right on Madison, then left on 15th Ave. After about a mile, turn right on Aloha for one block—Salisbury House is on the corner of 16th Ave East and Aloha.

SALISBURY HOUSE
Innkeepers: Mary & Cathryn Wiese
750 16th Avenue East
Seattle, WA 98112, USA
Tel: (206) 328-8682, Fax: (206) 720-1019
5 Rooms, Double: $125–$169
Open: all year, Credit cards: all major
www.karenbrown.com/salisburyhouse.html

We love the small lobby of this hotel—it's like old, scholarly Oxford or the working library of Sherlock Holmes, all in rich leather burgundies and golds, with built-in bookshelves, a fire, and oversized floral paintings in huge gold frames. Guestrooms, on the other hand, are decorated in a boutique style reminiscent of the Renaissance in rich color schemes of gold, pomegranate, royal blue, and green. Layered tapestries frame the beds and playful furniture is arranged for accent. All rooms are spacious and have fax machines, speakerphones with data ports, private bars, and televisions. Most face the Seattle streets, but a few face a neighboring building. One suite, the Château Ste. Michelle, is available, featuring a wood-burning fireplace, tiled step-up bathtub, granite vanity, jetted shower, and surround-sound stereo system. A vineyard theme is celebrated throughout, so each room is named for a different Washington winery. The concierge, Greg Frederick, is also a sommelier, so don't miss his complimentary wine receptions each evening or his late-night port service in the lobby living room. Dine in the cheerful, bustling Tulio, voted "Best Italian Restaurant in Seattle" by Seattle Magazine. *Directions:* From Seattle airport, take I-5 north to Seneca St. At the end of the off-ramp, veer left onto Seneca. Turn left on 5th Ave and stay in the left lane—the hotel is on the left at Spring St.

HOTEL VINTAGE PARK
Manager: Sandy Burkett
1100 Fifth Avenue
Seattle, WA 98101, USA
Tel: (206) 624-8000, Fax: (206) 623-0568
Toll Free: (888) 454-8401
126 Rooms, Double: $159–$229*
*Breakfast not included
Open: all year, Credit cards: all major
www.karenbrown.com/vintagepark.html

The Shelburne Inn is a step back to the late 19th century, at once stately, traditionally elegant and country casual. We felt as if we were aboard an ancient ship, walking the narrow carpeted hallways with their low ceilings and walls of tongue and groove. Bedrooms tend to be small; but are cozy and handsome, and each one is thoughtfully and uniquely decorated with enormous pieces of imposing antique furniture. Sometimes the wainscoting is painted in a soft shade of pink or blue or green; sometimes it's left in its natural state to complement a floral wallpaper. Most have claw-foot tubs with sunflower showerheads. In the lobby downstairs, a wood-burning fire glows warmly. It's here that Laurie and David serve their soul-warming breakfasts at a large oak table. You'll choose from several hot items on David's menu, and chances are he has smoked the salmon in your egg scramble or personally hunted outdoors for the mushrooms in your omelet. Laurie has baked the warm, fresh bread. Two more gently gracious hosts cannot be found. Dine at the casually sophisticated Shoalwater Restaurant dominated by stunning 19th-century Art Nouveau stained glass salvaged from a church in England. It bases its cuisine on an abundance of fresh, locally harvested foods and boasts one of the best wine lists in the world, according to Gourmet magazine. *Directions:* Take Hwy 101 north across the Astoria Bridge. Turn left to Ilwaco and drive 2 miles to Seaview.

SHELBURNE INN
Innkeepers: Laurie Anderson & David Campiche
4415 Pacific Way
P. O. Box 250
Seaview, WA 98644, USA
Tel: (360) 642-2442, Fax: (360) 642-8904
Toll Free: (800) 466-1896
15 Rooms, Double: $135–$195
Open: all year, Credit cards: all major
Select Registry
www.karenbrown.com/shelburne.html

The Lost Mountain Lodge sits in perfect harmony with its environment at the edge of the Olympic National Park. The gray-blue shingled building is surrounded by 6 lovely acres of trees, meadows, and ponds—a haven for both guests and wildlife. The interior is stunning: huge windows and an open-plan design with a 27-foot vaulted ceiling give a marvelous sense of space and light. Furnishings are tasteful and of the highest quality and the color scheme brings the outdoors inside with the willow green carpet echoing the color of the ponds. The complimentary hot & cold beverage center in the lovely kitchen is always open to guests. Overlooking the sitting room is a reading loft with comfortable chairs and a table for games. Guestrooms are sophisticated and luxurious. All have king beds, European duvets, sitting areas, wood-burning fireplaces, and excellent bathrooms. The Moonbeam enjoys large skylights in a vaulted ceiling, The Creekside has a wonderful spa-like bathroom, and The Sunnyview boasts a charming window-seat alcove. Out on the deck overlooking the ponds and waterfall, a hydrotherapy spa offers many different massage options. Two very child-friendly guesthouses offer well-equipped, comfortable self-catering accommodation. *Directions:* From the 101, turn south on Hooker Road and drive for just over a mile. Turn left into Sunny View Estates (Sunny View Drive) and follow it to the end. Bear right and take the first gravel road to your left.

LOST MOUNTAIN LODGE
Innkeepers: Dwight & Lisa Hostvedt
303 Sunny View Drive
Sequim, WA 98382, USA
Tel: (360) 683-2431, Fax: (360) 683-2996
Toll Free: (888) 683-2431
3 Rooms, Double: $185–$295
2 cottages: $295–$350
Breakfast served in Main Lodge only
Open: all year, Credit cards: MC, VS
www.karenbrown.com/lostmountain.html

Overlooking the awe-inspiring, 268-foot Snoqualmie Falls, Salish Lodge is positively extravagant. This place is stunning, with an interior designed like a private luxury vacation home. All bedrooms are classified deluxe and are handsomely decorated in woodsy tones of brown, black, red, and gold. Woodwork is custom-made and floors combine slate with lush carpets in Native American patterns. All rooms offer wood-burning fireplaces; as well as whirlpool tubs for two, Aveda toiletries, deep, feather beds, and . . . a pillow menu. Really. They've got pillows for pregnant women, pillows for bad backs, eye pillows, lavender pillows, buckwheat pillows—just ask. In the mornings, enjoy a guided walking tour down to the base of the falls, sacred ground to the Native Americans who once lived here. The Spa is a thoroughly tranquil spot, where Japan meets the Northwest in architectural beauty. Choose from two restaurants, both of which offer terrific views of the falls and surrounds. Our only word of caution is that Snoqualmie Falls is the second most popular tourist spot in Washington, so Salish can feel crowded in the public areas and restaurants, especially in summer months. *Directions:* From Seattle airport, take 405 north, then I-90 east towards Spokane. At Exit 25, turn left onto Snoqualmie Parkway, left on Railroad Avenue, then proceed ¼ mile. The Lodge is on your left.

SALISH LODGE & SPA
Manager: Sam Johnson
6501 Railroad Avenue SE
Snoqualmie, WA 98065, USA
Tel: (425) 888-2556, Fax: (425) 888-2533
Toll Free: (800) 826-6124
91 Rooms, Double: $229–$409*
*Breakfast not included
Open: all year, Credit cards: all major
www.karenbrown.com/salish.html

Tacoma, with its Dome entertainment complex, renowned Museum of Glass, and splendid new art museum, is becoming a popular tourist destination. Here, in a modest neighborhood on the southern edge of town, you can find comfortable accommodations in a 1911 Colonial-style mansion on the National Register of Historic Places. This was originally the home of Emma Smith DeVoe, a noted suffragette, whose photo is proudly displayed on a desk in the sitting room. This is a handsome, spacious room with dark-red walls; white woodwork; shuttered, lead-paned windows; black marble fireplace; and furniture appropriate to the period. Your enthusiastic and personable hosts, the Teifkes, are keen collectors of antiques, which you find throughout the house. The dining room and entry areas have rather vividly painted walls, but are charming nonetheless and have lovely oak floors. Upstairs, the four individually decorated bedrooms all have private bathrooms, antique or reproduction beds, fine linens, TVs with VCRs, and fluffy robes. Outside, the 1½ acres of pretty grounds create an in-town oasis. Renovation is ongoing: plans in hand when I visited were to remodel Carrie's Room to include a modern en suite bathroom and to add fireplaces to Emma's Room and Susan's Room. *Directions:* From I-5, go east on Hwy 512 approximately 2 miles to the Pacific Avenue exit. Turn right onto Pacific Avenue, then left on 133rd Street (about 2 miles), driving two blocks to the inn.

DEVOE MANSION
Innkeepers: Cheryl & Dave Teifke
208 133rd Street East
Tacoma, WA 98445, USA
Tel: (253) 539-3991, Fax: (253) 539-8539
Toll Free: (888) 539-3991
4 Rooms, Double: $115–$149
Open: all year, Credit cards: all major
www.karenbrown.com/devoe.html

A villa? In Tacoma? Well, yes—a 12,000-square-foot, historic Italian Renaissance villa, complete with white stucco exterior, red-tile roof and fountains surrounded by flower-filled gardens. Step into the entryway and into a fantasy, where enormous rooms are painted in peaceful colors; where high ceilings, an abundance of windows, massive fireplaces, and oversized furniture are standard. Guestrooms, all with tub and shower in the bathroom, some with private balconies, range from cozy to palatial; and your hosts will find the right fit and degree of privacy for you. Sorrento is fully 800 square feet with comfortable overstuffed sofas arranged in front of the gas fire, a king canopy bed, and a huge veranda. Amalfi and Casert have Jacuzzis and look out over the piazza with fountain or garden with reflection pool. Kristy and Aaron welcome you warmly and tend to the details that make for a wonderful stay: complimentary wine and beer, Portuguese damask sheets, and breakfast served at a large table with fresh flowers and candles. They even offer room service if requested. *Directions:* From I-5, take I-705 at Exit 133 to Tacoma. Follow signs for Shuster Parkway, then take the Stadium Way exit. Turn right onto Stadium, right on Tacoma Ave N, and left on N. 5th Street.

THE VILLA
Innkeepers: Kristy & Aaron House
705 N. 5th Street
Tacoma, WA 98403, USA
Tel: (253) 572-1157, Fax: none
Toll Free: (800) 572-1157
5 Rooms, Double: $145–$250
Open: all year, Credit cards: all major
www.karenbrown.com/villa.html

Travel & Leisure declared Cliff House one of the 50 "Most Romantic Places on Earth." This unique architectural wonder, set in a lush forest on the edge of Admiralty Inlet, is spectacular, sophisticated, and rustic. Soaring spaces alternate with cozy secluded nooks in a design that continuously surprises. You won't find a door in the place, except to conceal bathrooms. No matter where you are positioned, you find yourself engulfed by nature, both forest and water. Cliff House is a pure celebration of freedom and wide, open spaces. An enormous full kitchen is readied for your arrival: the refrigerator is stocked for breakfast and the table beautifully set. Linger in the sunken living room in front of a huge wood-burning fireplace. Cozy up in a solarium-like sitting area and enjoy a good book. Climb stairs to the master loft bedroom with king feather bed to take in the staggering view as you listen to the surf break below. Soak in a jetted tub. A low-ceilinged corner is filled with a collection of Native American and African art. Hike steps down to the beach or sit on the tree-house platform and watch the sunset. Also available for rent is the adorable and more affordable Cottage, decorated in rustic style and sporting whimsical murals in the bedroom and bathroom. *Directions:* From the Mukilteo ferry, take 525 north for about 10½ miles to Bush Point Road and turn left. Drive 1½ miles, turn left on Windmill, then follow signs to Cliff House.

CLIFF HOUSE AND COTTAGE
Innkeepers: Peggy Moore & Walter O'Toole
727 Windmill Drive
Whidbey Island—Freeland, WA 98249, USA
Tel: (360) 331-1566, Fax: none
Toll Free: (800) 297-4118
1 house: $450, 1 cottage: $195
Open: all year, Credit cards: none
www.karenbrown.com/cliffhouse.html

Nestled in the trees and with its deck jutting over the wildlife pond, The Lodge is the largest and most remarkable of six log cottages on 25 acres of woodland. Antiques handed down the family line as well as those from Mary Jane's collecting days, fill the space; including rarities like an old church collection box with coin slots labeled for different charities. Upstairs the loft space goes on and on, with a king-sized bed and two Jacuzzi tubs, one in a cozy corner under a skylight and a second overlooking the glass-enclosed living area below. Downstairs are a full kitchen, two sitting and two dining areas, a stone fireplace, and massive windows capturing the lovely, serene views. In the other cottages, wooded paths lead from one to the other, but you'd never know you had neighbors. All have about them the feeling of a cozy, rustic home in the Appalachian Mountains, complete with rocking porches and names like The Kentucky and Emma Jane's Tennessee. They are self-sufficient, island homes with full kitchens. To add to a welcoming "lived in" quality, all are readied for your arrival: the river-rock fireplace is ready to light, the table is set, the lights are on, and the pantry is full. Guests enjoy the use of a small exercise room, and a swimming pool and hot tub surrounded by lawn and flowers. This is the perfect choice for a peaceful getaway. *Directions:* From the Mukilteo ferry, take Hwy 525 about 16 miles north to the Guest House sign on your left.

GUEST HOUSE LOG COTTAGES
Innkeeper: Mary Jane Creger
24371 State Route 525
Whidbey Island—Greenbank, WA 98253, USA
Tel & Fax: (360) 678-3115
Toll Free: (800) 997-3115
6 Cottages, Double: $130–$325
Open: all year, Credit cards: MC, VS
www.karenbrown.com/guesthouse.html

These three cottages, situated 100 feet above a rocky beach on 6½ acres of lush green lawn, woods, and fairy-tale garden, with sweeping views of Saratoga Passage, will tug permanently at your soul. Gray whales feed on shrimp in coves below. Eagles perch in trees overhead. Sunsets stop your heart. Dove House is essentially your own private two-level lodge with romantic loft bedroom, second room with bunk beds, river-rock fireplace, outdoor hot tub, and full kitchen. Chauntecleer House, another two-story hideaway, is closest to the bluff's edge and furnished in a contemporary country style. It has a full kitchen with bay window, an open fireplace, a large bedroom with skylight, its own hot tub, and a private deck. Finally, there's The Potting Shed, an enchanting secret garden of a place, nearly concealed under canopies of clematis. It has a queen bed with separate sitting room, a wood-burning stove, a large bath with two-person jetted tub and shower, and a full kitchen. You find lavish and artful attention to quality and detail throughout in the tile, the woodwork, the linens, the flatware, the creative use of space. These dreamlike places provide the ultimate in a tranquil, private retreat. *Directions:* From the Mukilteo ferry, take 525 north for 3 miles, then turn right on Langley Rd. At the stop sign just after the school, turn right on Cascade, then left on 2nd Street, which becomes Saratoga Rd. The property is on the right, about half a mile from the village.

DOVE HOUSE, CHAUNTECLEER HOUSE,
THE POTTING SHED
Innkeepers: Bunny & Bob Meals
5081 Saratoga Road, P.O. Box 659
Whidbey Island—Langley, WA 98260, USA
Tel: (360) 221-5494, Fax: (360) 221-8230
Toll Free: (800) 637-4436
3 Cottages, Double: $200–$325
Open: all year, Credit cards: all major
www.karenbrown.com/dove.html

Offering exceptional value, Eagles Nest—a Registered Backyard Wildlife Sanctuary—is a panoramic, forested haven adjacent to 400 acres of wooded trails. The first common room you enter is constructed similar to a lodge with towering ceilings, a small wood-burning fireplace, and a grand piano. Ascend the first flight of stairs to the Saratoga Room with terrific views of land and sea. The Forest Room will make you feel as though you are in the woods, as you look out through large windows and skylights. Both offer king-sized beds, private decks or balconies, and are pleasant in their decor. No expense is spared on the comfortable beds with fine linens and down comforters. Also on this floor is a second, spacious sitting room with comfortable chairs, a wet bar, bookshelves, Indian art, and a deer head mounted high on the wall. The final flight of stairs leads directly into the most dramatic spot in the place: the Eagles Nest Room, cleverly shaped as an octagon with as many windows to command a 360-degree view of Saratoga Passage, Camano Island, and Mt. Baker. On the ground level, below the main entrance, is the Garden Suite, a pleasant hideaway decorated in pinks, yellows, and blues. A large hot tub is available on grounds for guests. *Directions:* From the Mukilteo ferry, take 525 north. Turn right on Langley Road, right on Cascade, and left on 2nd St. which becomes Saratoga. Continue almost 1½ miles on Saratoga—there are signs to the inn on the left.

EAGLES NEST INN
Innkeepers: Jerry & Joanne Lechner
4680 Saratoga Road
Whidbey Island—Langley, WA 98260, USA
Tel & Fax: (360) 221-5331
Toll Free: (800) 243-5536
4 Rooms, Double: $95–$160
2 night minimum on weekends
Open: all year, Credit cards: MC, VS
www.karenbrown.com/eaglesnest.html

For a dose of contemporary sophistication in the heart of this island town, the Inn at Langley is the place. This modern complex of handsome guestrooms, rather like sleek beach apartments, is situated so that every guestroom takes in a 180-degree view of Puget Sound and the majestic Cascades. Rooms are decorated minimally, in ways reminiscent of Japan. Bathrooms, for example, have a handsomely tiled open shower equipped with a wooden stool for washing, and an adjacent soaking tub that looks to the water through a large open window. Pocket doors that separate bathrooms from bedrooms, and bedrooms from sitting rooms, are made with opaque glass framed in wood, reminiscent of shoji screens. It makes for a very rejuvenating, serene atmosphere. All rooms, whether standards or suites, have fireplaces and wonderful, expanded, porch-style balconies. They're decorated in quiet tones, with beautiful slate accents and leather sofas. At the water's edge is a stone fire pit—a romantic place to settle. The dining room is huge with an open kitchen; a massive, two-sided, river-rock fireplace; and French doors opening onto a lovely patio and herb garden. An extended Continental breakfast is served here each morning, and a six-course dinner is available on Fridays and Saturdays. *Directions:* From the Mukilteo ferry, take 525 north for 3 miles, then turn right on Langley Rd. At the stop sign, go right onto Cascade Avenue, which turns into First St.

INN AT LANGLEY
Innkeepers: Paul & Pam Schell
400 First Street
PO Box 835
Whidbey Island—Langley, WA 98260, USA
Tel & Fax: (360) 221-3033
24 Rooms, Double: $265–$495
2 cottages
Dinner served Fri and Sat only
Open: all year, Credit cards: all major
www.karenbrown.com/langley.html

If you are more comfortable in a traditional hotel than in, say, a more adventurous island accommodation, Saratoga Inn is a good choice. This attractive, two-story, Cape Cod-style building with wraparound porch has a great location at the top of a bluff overlooking the water and is located conveniently in town. Downstairs, guests can enjoy a two-sided gas fireplace that divides a small sitting room, with lots of windows, from a small dining area. A Four Sister's Inn, a buffet table in the latter is spread each morning with a full breakfast of hot and cold selections, and again in the afternoon with wine, cheese, and other special items made right on the premises. Though the inn itself is small, bedrooms are plenty sizeable with large windows. In design, they are contemporary, elegant, and cheerful. The upstairs rooms have high ceilings and the best views. Many have window seats—and a teddy bear, of course. All have gas fireplaces, color televisions, phones with data ports, and sparkling bathrooms with oversized, tiled showers. You'll definitely want a room with a water view. The private Carriage House offers 650 square feet of privacy with its own kitchen, a king sleigh bed, claw-foot tub, fireplace, and deck overlooking the water. *Directions:* From the Mukilteo ferry, drive north on 525 for 3 miles, then turn right on Langley Road. At the stop sign just after the school at the edge of town, turn right on Cascade—the inn is on the left at the corner of Second.

SARATOGA INN
Manager: Cheryl Lambour
201 Cascade Avenue
P.O. Box 428
Whidbey Island—Langley, WA 98260, USA
Tel: (360) 221-5801, Fax: (360) 221-5804
Toll Free: (800) 698-2910
16 Rooms, Double: $125–$300
Open: all year, Credit cards: all major
www.karenbrown.com/saratoga.html

At Sun Mountain Lodge, tranquility, activity, and service come together in a winning combination. Graciously residing on 3,000 mountainous acres, this handsome hotel captures stirring views of Gardner Mountain and the majestic Cascades. Guest accommodations occupy three unique buildings. In the main lodge, rooms are decorated in a rustically elegant style to complement the lodge itself, with a charming mix of rough-hewn wood, rock, plush carpet, and custom light fixtures in warm tones of brown, tan, and gold. Boardwalks, wood pillars, and massive stonework make the Gardner building an imposing one. Rooms here offer gas fireplaces, a separate sitting area, beautiful bathrooms, and a stereo system. In the neighboring Mt. Robinson building, rooms are equipped with jetted tubs and finished in black lacquered wood, iron, and willow. The formal dining room retains its original architectural charm. Lighter fare can be had in the adjacent Wolf Creek Bar and Grill. From the outdoor swimming pools and hot tubs, you feel as though you could touch the mountains. Over 100 miles of neighboring trails will entice you to hike, bike, fish, horse ride, or ski. Whether you decide to stay close to the grounds or explore the neighboring wilderness, Sun Mountain Lodge will rejuvenate. *Directions:* Headed south through town on Hwy 20, cross the bridge, turn right on Twin Lakes Road, and right on Patterson Lake Road for 3 miles.

SUN MOUNTAIN LODGE
Manager: Brian Charlton
604 Patterson Lake Road, P.O. Box 1000
Winthrop, WA 98862, USA
Tel: (509) 996-2211, Fax: (509) 996-3133
Toll Free: (800) 572-0493
97 Rooms, Double: $200–$450*
16 cottages: $300–$750
*Breakfast not included: $18
Open: all year, Credit cards: all major
www.karenbrown.com/sun.html

On 5 rural acres in the Sammamish River Valley, next door to Château Ste. Michelle and Columbia wineries and only 20 miles northeast of Seattle, Willows Lodge is one of Northwest's luxury lodges—and we mean high-tech luxury: 27-inch TVs, DVD players, showers with digital temperature controls, beautiful glass light fixtures with elaborate dimming capabilities, and high-speed internet access. Suites offer Bang & Olufsen stereo systems with surround sound! If your refrigerator is empty, it's only until you've had the time to submit an order to re-stock it. Rooms are beautifully decorated in a restful blend of wood and slate, with stone fireplaces, high ceilings, large windows, and private patios or decks, capturing the contemporary feel of a fine hotel and the Northwest informality of a lodge. Beds and baths offer an embarrassment of riches: sinks of Mexican marble, Australian lambs wool mattress pads, down duvets, and Italian linens. Two superb restaurants are located on the grounds: the marvelous, award-winning Barking Frog, and the nationally acclaimed Herbfarm, which offers superb nine-course meals showcasing the best of Northwest cuisine. Willows Lodge is class, class, class. *Directions:* From Seattle, take I-5 north to 90 east to 405 north. At Exit 20B, turn right on 124th, left on 132nd, and right on 143rd. Stay to the right and proceed past the stop sign on NE 145th Street. Willows Lodge is on your left just past the Redhook Brewery.

WILLOWS LODGE
General Manager: Tom Waithe
14580 NE 145th Street
Woodinville, WA 98072, USA
Tel: (425) 424-3900, Fax: (425) 424-2585
Toll Free: (877) 424-3930
86 Rooms, Double: $265–$755
Open: all year, Credit cards: all major
www.karenbrown.com/willows.html

Index

215

KAREN BROWN wrote her first travel guide in 1976. Her personalized travel series has grown to 17 titles, which Karen and her small staff work diligently to keep updated. Karen, her husband, Rick, and their children, Alexandra and Richard, live in Moss Beach, a small town on the coast south of San Francisco. They settled here in 1991 when they opened Seal Cove Inn. Karen is frequently traveling but when she is home, in her role as innkeeper, enjoys welcoming Karen Brown readers.

JUNE EVELEIGH BROWN'S love of travel was inspired by the *National Geographic* magazines that she read as a girl in her dentist's office—so far she has visited over 40 countries. June hails from Sheffield, England, and lived in Zambia and Canada before moving to northern California where she lives in San Mateo with her husband, Tony, their daughter, Clare, their two German Shepherds, and a Siamese cat.

BETH KNUTSEN spent several soul-starved years in high tech before hitting the open road. A great lover of travel and an aficionado of the charming bed and breakfast scene, Beth continued the Karen Brown tradition of discovering the most charming accommodations in the Pacific Northwest.

JANN POLLARD, The artist of the cover painting has studied art since childhood, and is well known for her outstanding impressionistic-style watercolors. Jann's original paintings are represented through The Gallery in Burlingame, CA and New Masters Gallery in Carmel, CA. *www.jannpollard.com.* Fine art giclée prints of her paintings are available at *www.karenbrown.com.*

VANESSA KALE produced all of the property sketches and itinerary illustrations in this guide. A native of Bellingham, Washington, Vanessa spent her high school year in Sonoma California. After graduating in Art from U.C. Davis, Vanessa moved to southern California where she lives with her husband, Simon. She works as a project manager for an architectural rendering company, and also as a freelance artist. *www.vanessakale.com.*

Notes

Watch for a New Thriller Series
Featuring "Karen Brown"
As Travel Writer & Undercover Sleuth

Author M. Diane Vogt, the creator of the critically acclaimed and popular Judge Wilhelmina Carson legal suspense novels, is writing a new series featuring the exploits of "Karen Brown".

Combine the heroic salvage consultant Travis McGee – from John D. MacDonald's hugely successful Ft. Lauderdale mystery/thriller series with *Under the Tuscan Sun's* Frances Mayes, and that's Karen Brown, clandestine recovery specialist and world renowned travel writer.

Based on actual places and destinations as featured in Karen Brown's guides, join Karen in her travels as by day she inspects charming hotels, and by night she dabbles in intrigue and defeats the world of killers, scoundrels, and scam artists.

The series has been launched with the publication of James Patterson's best selling book, *Thriller*. The short story, "Surviving Toronto" introduces sleuth, Karen Brown.

Awards coming soon......

Reader feedback will be used to evaluate and award exceptional quality and service for Karen Brown Recommended Properties.

Quality

Service

On our website Karen Brown Travelers will have the ability to vote for a property in a number of categories, including but not limited to; best breakfast, location/setting, welcome, comfort/ambiance, value, and romance.

KAREN · BROWN
KB
20 07
·BEST·

Ambiance

Karen Brown Presents Her Own Special Hideaways

Karen Brown's Seal Cove Inn

Spectacularly set amongst wildflowers and bordered by cypress trees, Seal Cove Inn (Karen's second home) looks out to the distant ocean. Each room has a fireplace, cozy sitting area, and a view of the sea. Located on the coast, 35 minutes south of San Francisco.

Seal Cove Inn, Moss Beach, California
toll free telephone: (800) 995-9987
www.sealcoveinn.com

Karen Brown's Dolphin Cove Inn

Hugging a steep hillside overlooking the sparkling deep-blue bay of Manzanillo, Dolphin Cove Inn offers guests outstanding value. Each room has either a terrace or a balcony, and a breathtaking view of the sea. Located on the Pacific Coast of Mexico.

Dolphin Cove Inn, Manzanillo, Mexico
toll free telephone: (866) 360-9062
www.dolphincoveinn.com